Good morning, how are you? As if I cared...
No likey Oh crikey
Lovely grub, lovely grub!
I always do my best for all my gentlemen.
I wish I had as many shillings—
Good morning! Nice day.
Mr. Handley!
Can I do you now, sir?
Ain't it a shame, eh— ain't it a shame...
After you, Claude. No—after you, Cecil—
This is Funf speaking—

That's the boy!
Most irregular most irregular
ut I'm all right now...
No CUPS OUTSIDE!
t's being so cheerful as keeps me going...
I don't mind if I do—
I go— I come back
Notting at all, notting at all...
What's concentrated cacophony?
T.T.F.N.
Well, for evermore!

Scripts by Ted Kavanagh
Introduction by P J Kavanagh

The Itma Years

Reminiscences by Maurice Denham
Deryck Guyler
Hattie Jacques
Molly Weir
Clarence Wright
Fred Yule

Drawings by Horner

Futura Publications Limited

A Futura book

First published in Great Britain in 1974
by The Woburn Press

First Futura Publications edition 1975
published in association with
The Woburn Press

ISBN: 0 8600 7245 2

Futura Publications Limited
49 Poland Street, London W1A 2LG

THE ITMA YEARS

Other titles in this series of classics
of broadcasting comedy include:

ROUND THE HORNE
HANCOCK'S HALF HOUR
THE BEST OF MORECAMBE AND WISE

The Publishers acknowledge with thanks
the co-operation of the BBC

Acknowledgements are also due to the
following organizations for their permission
to reproduce copyright illustrations:
Ascherberg, Hopwood & Crew Ltd. –
page 14 (*ITMA Rhymes*);
BBC Pictorial Publicity – pages 18, 20
(*top left, bottom left, middle right*), 38, 40
(*middle left*), 64, 66 (*bottom right*), 88, 90,
114, 116, 136, 138;
Daily Mirror – page 157;
The Imperial War Museum – page 40
(*middle right*);
Keystone – pages 20 (*bottom right*), 40
(*bottom left*), 66 (*top right, middle right*);
Radio Times – page 13 (*cartoon, Tom
Marches Back*), 40 (*top left*), 66 (*middle left*);
Radio Times Hulton Picture Library –
page 20 (*top right*).
The ration book on page 40 is reproduced
by permission of the Controller, H.M.S.O.
The reproduction from *Radio Fun* on page
14 appears by kind permission of I.P.C.
Juvenile Magazines.
The publishers would also like to thank
Brian Doyle, Denis Gifford, and BBC
Sound Archives for their co-operation.
Sources for the linking material were
Tommy Handley by Ted Kavanagh
(Hodder & Stoughton, 1949) and *ITMA
1939-1948* by Francis Worsley (Vox Mundi
Ltd., 1948).

Introduction

The ITMA years, 1939-49, were the years of my childhood, so my account has to be personal, childlike, the history of my father and my family seen from the inside and as it were, from below.

My first conscious *thought* about my father's strange work—for surely the manufacture of jokes, by the week, is an unusual occupation—was that there must be easier ways of earning a living. We were in Bristol and the house next door had been bombed and set on fire. In fact it was a smoking hole and its disappearance had exposed the side wall of the house we lived in, behind which my father sat writing, also smoking, his enormous domed forehead in his pudgy hand, his equally fat fountain pen in the other, covering sheets of blue-lined foolscap. On the other side of the wall, now, as I say, an outside wall, which it had not been when we had gone to bed last night in the cellar, firemen played their hoses to stop it cracking. It steamed gently, and perhaps to a clairvoyant eye my father's joke-brewing dome was steaming too. I don't know whether I thought then, but I certainly think now, that his job was much harder than that of the journalist who must write of what he sees and experiences. He, on the contrary, not only had to ignore what was happening but had to write as though it hadn't happened, churning out this week's laughs. I seem to remember at this time he was writing a show called 'Send for Doctor Dick', or it may have been 'Lucky Dip', for in 1940 he was a hard-ridden hack and the BBC had not yet realised that ITMA could be allowed to consume all his energies and would, in future days, be something upon which it could preen itself. At this time I think he was writing two or three shows a week and was paid ten pounds. However, there had been periods of unemployment before this, times were hard and likely to get harder, and he was enjoying himself; he always did although, like any sensible man, he detested work.

He was of a very curious appearance. The best way I can express it is to say that, as more time passes, I become progressively conscious that I have never seen anyone who remotely resembles him. There have been other red-haired, stout men, balding, thick

Introduction

of neck, with spade-like fingers, small hands and small feet. There have been other little, red moustaches. But not in that particular combination. Not nearly. Everyone else has a double, or someone you can nearly greet in the street until you realise your mistake. But not him. He certainly wasn't handsome, but nor could you call him ugly. He was in the true sense distinguished, because he was so distinctive. At home and on holiday careless of his dress, for the streets he was almost a dandy; when in funds he used to wear some discreetly splendid tweed suits. I loved his smart preparations for the out-of-doors, it was always the best time to ask him for money. He was brisk, cheerful and full of anticipation of what the town had to hold. It was very nearly impossible to imagine him in the country.

How does a man start, as a comedy scriptwriter. Well, in this case my father, of Irish stock, came from New Zealand to Edinburgh to study medicine. The First World War intervened, he went into the Army, afterwards did various jobs, writing advertisements for Burroughs Wellcome, cartoon scripts, etc. He was a keen whisker-twiddler on the old crystal radio sets, one day heard a comedian he liked, sent him a sketch, the comedian (T. Handley) bought it, and so their long association began. How ITMA started is a longer and more complex story, but briefly, like so many ideas that are found to work, it grew out of a series of half-cock ideas that didn't work at all. The outbreak of war was the catalyst. It was a time of officialdom and officiousness, that curious strain of self-importance that a crisis brings out in certain of the British was ripe for deflation, and Tommy Handley, with the voice of a disaster-prone con-man, more bent than a six pound note and cheery with it, was the ideal man to do the deflating. It was a time of pompous initials also, A.R.P., L.D.V., and so on; Tommy doodled on a piece of paper I t's T hat M an A gain, and ITMA was born.

Basically, there were three men involved and as my father points out in his book on Tommy Handley, none of them could have managed without the others: comedian, producer, writer. And the fourth participant, as important as any other, was the War. The nation blacked-out, apprehensive, with nothing whatsoever to entertain it except a comparatively new toy, the radio.

His private relations with Tommy Handley are difficult to define. Although they were friendly—very—it would be difficult to call them friends. Outside working hours they hardly met. They were both very private men, but in different ways. Whereas my father's world was one of pubs and clubs (where a man in the midst of a crowd can be as private as he pleases, all the more so if he is their accredited jokesmith) Tommy Handley liked to go home and read—at least that's what everybody presumed he did there, nobody knew for certain. Generous with his time and his extreme geniality (to the point of psychic exhaustion, which is probably what killed him), he was careful of his privacy and his money. No back-slapping, no rounds of drinks for the boys, he was either on-stage, in the public eye, or invisible, gone. On-stage, and I mean it in the general sense, in the middle of a crowd of admirers as well as actually performing, I found him, as a child, adorable. He was very funny indeed, with plenty of time, and special jokes, for me and for all the other fringe members of any group, barmen,

Introduction

commissionaires, bores. It's true that sometimes, in the midst of all the laughter, my father looked a little wan. But then, it was only natural, he was bound to have heard some part of it all before. Tommy was handsome, almost in a leading-mannish sort of way, but there was a tell-tale crinkle at the corners of the eyes that mocked the effect of his electric presence even while he included you inside it. He stood outside himself, he had style, in any company or profession he would have been a star. Like all great performers he shone in the radiance of his effect on others. No-one who had ever met him would call him 'only' a radio comedian, as though that is a minor form of art. Perhaps it is, but there was nothing minor about his presence.

The third member of the triumvirate was the producer, Francis Worsley, pipe-smoking, corduroy-jacketed, schoolmasterly. Any producer's role is difficult to describe but it's probably true to say that he held the three of them together. Without Tommy the words wouldn't have meant much and without Francis my father wouldn't have gone on producing the words. I remember him standing at my father's bedside taking an overdue script from him sheet by sheet as, groaning, my father scribbled it.

Some other members of the cast are still vivid from my childhood. Dino Galvani (Signor So-So) who even in real life was very much the stage-Italian, gentle, wistful. I remember him holding out his hands, gnarled with arthritis, and elegiacally remembering his matinée idol days: 'I used to pick ze ladies like ploms off ze trees—ploms off ze trees.' Horace Percival (Ali Oop, the Diver, Claude), lantern-jawed, immaculate story-teller, shakily coming down to breakfast at a provincial hotel after too long a session the previous night, and to my fascination using his tie as a sort of pulley to steady his tomato juice on its uncertain progress towards his mouth. Sydney Keith (Sam Scram), small, spectacled, and like the old musical comedy man he was, suddenly grabbing my delighted, blushing nine-year-old self and doing a soft-shoe shuffle with me across the stage of a freezing cinema in Bangor during a rehearsal. Fred Yule (Chief Bigga Banga), vast baritone, who in my father's opinion one day somewhat over-discussed his ailments. So he said, 'Come on Fred, have a pint of pus with me'. (Invited by someone to lunch at Simpson's my father was disappointed to discover it was Simpson's the clothes shop in Piccadilly, not Simpson's in the Strand. So he ordered a boiled shirt.) Jack Train (Colonel Chinstrap), who always had a new gadget to show us, and who used to take us for drives in his car, a great treat in those days of petrol rationing. Friendly, chirpy Jean Capra (Poppy Poopah) and Clarrie Wright (*Good morning, nice* day!). That's what I remember about them all, extreme friendliness to each other and to a doubtless boring child. For the rest of my life I will love showbiz people, who are usually thought so steely, so self-seeking. That has not been my experience. It was all indeed a team, the secretaries Joyce Walters, Teeny Goss, the performers, Tommy, my father, Francis, there was a family feeling, because of the war, because of being twice evacuated, the shared hotels, digs, discomforts, privations. And I couldn't help noticing that as far as I could tell they all seemed to love my father.

For me these scripts contain him, as well as the particular trick of voice that made Tommy Handley so cheeky, so friendly, so unpompous. I remember my father being

Introduction

rather pleased when an M.P., I think it was Bessie Braddock, described ITMA as 'a welter of bad puns'. He loved puns, alliterations, all forms of playing with the sound and meaning of words. So did Tommy. They must have had great fun.

One thing ITMA can take credit for, a loosening of the bonds of the possible in radio, characters entering without preamble, for no reason at all, and disappearing as fast. The speed was new, easily accepted by ear, it would have been more difficult to follow by eye. It bred a new style of comedy—perhaps a new style.

So it went on, year after year, the relations of the three central figures remaining the same and as friendly as ever; changes of cast but still the same atmosphere. You could feel it when you went to a rehearsal, and it came across in the broadcast. My father still leaving the script to the last moment, getting up at five in the morning, switching on the electric fire and working, smoking, still the brass ashtray, the fat fountain pen, so that by the time I got up the floor would be littered with foolscap and my father would keep wandering into the kitchen, chuckling, reading out bits. I'm not sure I laughed enough, or at all. My mother always did. But I hadn't yet realised that even grown-up Daddies need all the encouragement they can get. Then Tommy died. My father was very shaken, it had been a long partnership; in its own way, and because of the hugger-mugger conditions of the war, an intense one. But he said he felt he'd been released from a life sentence. More than three hundred scripts—it doesn't bear thinking of. He never found another tongue that could wrap itself round his words, or words he could shape around another tongue.

That unique tongue is now still, so is the fat fountain pen. Do the words on the pages that follow still have speed, flavour, reality? They certainly had plenty of those things once. Well, time alone knows. Or, as the clock said, T.O.K.

T.T.F.N.

P. J. Kavanagh
1974

ITMANIA

'A Mr. Funf would like to speak to you, sir'

Mrs HANDLEY'S BOY
'TOM
MARCHES BACK'
to a War Factory (Somewhere in England)
TOMMY HANDLEY
brings ITMA characters old and new
Script by Ted Kavanagh
Produced by Francis Worsley
WELL-FOR EVERMORE!

IT'S THAT MAN AGAIN

STARRING

TOMMY HANDLEY
WITH
GRETA GYNT · JACK TRAIN
and the ITMA COMPANY playing their Radio Characters

THE RADIO SENSATION with
TWENTY MILLION LISTENERS

Directed by WALTER FORDE

A GAINSBOROUGH

ITMANIA

In the early autumn of 1939 Tommy Handley's voice was a familiar one to many Britons. A master of fast patter, he had begun his career in concert-party and revue, but it was his broadcasting debut in 1925 which signalled the direction his talents were to take. Radio was ideally suited to his quick-fire approach, and wisely he allowed his own techniques to be further developed by the particular demands of the new medium. When the BBC Variety Department was looking for a comic anchorman for a series to follow the successful 'Bandwaggon' format of a comedy show with a storyline, broadcast weekly, Tommy Handley was the logical choice.

'It's That Man Again' had had a pilot run of four broadcasts in the summer of '39. Originally conceived by programme planners as an anglicised version of the Burns and Allen Show in the United States, the idea was discarded at an early stage and it was left to producer Francis Worsley, scriptwriter Ted Kavanagh and Handley himself to decide upon a format and theme. They chose to set the programmes on a broadcasting ship from which Handley, questionably assisted by his secretary Cilly (Celia Eddy) and a frenzied Russian inventor (Eric Egan), could send out any programmes to his liking. This was a reversal of the official situation at the time, when considerable caution over political jokes was necessitated by mounting international tension. The title for the radio show which was to produce more catchphrases than any other was itself taken from one of the moment. It was a Daily Express headline used each time Hitler staked yet another territorial claim, and increasingly on the lips of an apprehensive public.

The summer run was not particularly successful, but by the time the first programme of the new series was broadcast—19 September 1939—war had been declared and the mood of the nation had changed. ITMA appeared on the schedule as a thirty-minute comedy show included in the 120 hours of weekly broadcasting which the Variety Department, now in Bristol, had to produce. Handley, Kavanagh, and Worsley all felt that the series should lampoon Europe at war and create a zany atmosphere in which listeners could find relief from the anxieties of the time. The declaration of war had

spawned, seemingly overnight, a number of vast new ministries, teeming with government officials of varying degrees of importance and daily issuing orders to a baffled
populace. It was decided that That Man should join the growing ranks of officialdom
in a senior capacity, and so it was that Tommy Handley became the Minister of
Aggravation and Mysteries, c/o the Office of Twerps.

He was aided in his work by his secretary Dotty (Vera Lennox), Mrs Tickle the
office char and Vodkin the Russian inventor (Maurice Denham), and Fusspot (Jack
Train)—an unimaginative civil servant who, not surprisingly, found all of the Minister's
instructions 'most irregular'. Each programme included a parody of Radio Luxembourg
(which had stopped broadcasting with the outbreak of war)—Maurice Denham
announced for Radio Fakenburg and Sam Costa sang the commercials—while the
traditional music breaks and Michael North's signature tune were played by Jack
Hylton's Band, with Billy Ternent conducting. The second programme of the series
produced Jack Train's Funf, the elusive but omnipresent enemy spy. Perhaps the most
memorable character in this series, Funf became the helpless butt of Handley's jokes
and served to reduce the powerful German propaganda machine to little more than,
as Kavanagh put it, a radio joke. In November the Office of Twerps was evacuated to
the country and Handley encountered the additional task of dealing with the inhabitants
of a rural village, most notably Farmer Jollop (Jack Train).

By now the format was well-established: Handley supposedly trying to get on with
a new plan as Minister, constantly interrupted by the phone or a knock on the famous
ITMA door, entrance cues for the characters and catchphrases that plagued the
Minister's life. With cinemas and theatres closed down and increasing blackout
restrictions, the series attracted a ready audience (it was later to grow to more than
sixteen million listeners weekly), and it wasn't long before 'I wish I had as many
shillings' and 'I always do my best for all my gentlemen' had become an integral part of
everyday conversation.

Maurice Denham

Alias
Mrs Tickle
Vodkin
Announcer, Radio Fakenburg

Remembers

In 1939, just before war was declared, the BBC Repertory Company (about fourteen Variety Artistes and Actors with the BBC Chorus and some Orchestras) descended on Bristol. Among the many broadcasts we did each week was the first series of 'It's That Man Again', as ITMA was then called.

The live broadcasts were made from the Clifton Parish Hall, one of the various Church halls scattered about Bristol which had been hastily turned into studios. We would rehearse all afternoon from scripts that had been passed by Special Security. We had already been vetted by MI5 or some such before being permitted to broadcast. No departure was allowed from these scripts—in fact there was a gentleman in the control room with a button he could push to take the programme off the air if there was the slightest alteration. This was, of course, very frustrating for Tommy Handley, who was the master of ad-libbers, and Ted Kavanagh who couldn't change the scripts in rehearsal.

We were allowed, though, to make extremely derogatory remarks about Hitler and Goering etc.; this at first came as quite a shock as before war was declared we had always had to refer to them with careful deference!

I had the pleasant task in the broadcasts of playing all sorts of parts that cropped up in the scripts, including my main character of 'Mrs Lola Tickle', Tommy's first charlady whose catchphrase was 'I always do my best for all my gentlemen'. (In the stage show Tommy sometimes used to greet me as 'Tess', which always got a rude laugh from some of the quicker minded gentlemen (?) in the audience!) I also played 'Vodkin', a Russian inventor, the announcer at Tommy's radio station called Radio Fakenburg, an assortment of animals, and helped with effects.

This first series started the catchphrase 'This is Funf speaking', which was spoken by Jack Train sideways into a tumbler. It very quickly caught on and was used as the beginning of innumerable telephone calls throughout the British Isles.

I don't think that anyone concerned with the programme at that time realised that this was the start of a series that was to become essential listening all through the war and after, and that was to make Tommy Handley into a much-loved national figure.

The weekly broadcasts went on until February 1940 when we went out on a tour of the Music Halls with a stage version of the show. I found it very exciting to rush out on to the huge stage in 'drag' as Mrs Lola Tickle with my mop and bucket and play right out to the vast audiences in the various Hippodromes and Empires, as previously I had only played in straight plays in the confines of a stage set. This show included Tommy's well-known Music Hall sketch 'The Disorderly Room', in which I played the Sergeant-Major.

I think the only recording that exists of that first series is of a relay from the stage of the Palace Theatre, Manchester in May 1940, which happened to be my last performance in the show. I had got my Army call-up papers that week.

The collaboration of writer Ted Kavanagh (*left*), comedian Tommy Handley (*above left*), and producer Francis Worsley (*right*) was to sustain ITMA throughout its ten year run. Final alterations to the scripts were made in conference the day before transmission (*above right*).

With the declaration of war in September 1939, thousands of children were evacuated from the major urban centres. These London schoolchildren (*right*) are leaving Euston for the relative safety of the country.

Tommy Handley

in

It's That Man Again

(No. 13 Second series—No. 17)
Transmission
Tuesday, 12th December 1939, 7.35-8.05 p.m.
Home Service

ANNOUNCER   This is the BBC Home Service. 'It's That Man Again!'

TRIO & BAND   It's that man again,
Yes, that man again,
Yes sir, Tommy Handley is here.
You know the guy
He plays 'I spy'
With Furtive Funf —
Here's mud in his eye.

Mother's pride and joy
Mrs Handley's boy,
Oh, it's useless to complain —
When trouble's brewing, it's his doing,
That man, that man again.

TOMMY HANDLEY   Hello folks. 'It's That Man Again' and what a man. My name today is on the tip of everyone's tongue and the toe of everyone's boot. Why, I can't go out in the open these days without people shouting 'Heil Itma'! Some say 'Good old Itma' and others 'There goes the old blast-furnace' or words to that effect. I have been evacuated now for three weeks — three weeks of high jinks and low pranks. We've been very busy in the Office of Twerps though —

making out official forms and scribbling all over them, issuing orders one day and cancelling them the next. And the things we've written on the walls! Talk about one rood, pole or perch! My female staff have been extremely busy knitting me a pair of the most gorgeous galoshes you ever saw and now they're working on a surprise they're going to give me at Christmas — a shockproof waterproof and under-proof Funf-protector. There's been no sign or sound of Funf during the week and I must admit that I'm seriously concerned when I fail to hear from him — especially at night. That's when I suffer badly from Funf-starvation. My band has also improved since they've been put out to grass so I'll just let them sow a few wild notes just to prove it. What are you going to play, boys?

BAND	'Apple for the Teacher'.
TOMMY HANDLEY	'Apple for the Teacher'. Who's singing it?
BAND	June Malo.
TOMMY HANDLEY	June Malo — right, take a bite, June, and save me the chorus.
JUNE MALO & BAND	**'APPLE FOR THE TEACHER'**
TOMMY HANDLEY	Now let me see — what's been laid on my desk this morning. A duck egg, two dicarbicated cotton cow-cakes and a blue paper tied with red tape. I wonder what it can be? Ah — the plans of my secret broadcasting station. I must sit down to consider them.
Maurice Denham	*(dog yelping)*
TOMMY HANDLEY	Well muzzle mastaff that dog of mine in my chair again. Here, Isosceles. I'm the only one that's allowed to sleep in that chair.
Maurice Denham	*(as dog)* Funf to you.
TOMMY HANDLEY	Go and take your tail for a ta-ta. Now, I must examine these plans . . . .
F/X	**HAMMERING THROUGH WALL**
TOMMY HANDLEY	Nice quiet place this.
F/X	**DOOR OPENS**
TOMMY HANDLEY	Hello — what do you want? Oh — you're the man who's come to lay the telephone on.
MAN (Jack Train)	Oomph.

TOMMY HANDLEY	Well get on with it. How long is it going to take you?
MAN	Oomph.
TOMMY HANDLEY	Can't you do it any quicker?
MAN	Oomph — oomph.
TOMMY HANDLEY	Nice chatty little fellow, isn't he?
F/X	**HAMMERING CONTINUES**
TOMMY HANDLEY	Make less noise there. I must have peace to consider this blueprint.
F/X	**DOOR OPENS**
TOMMY HANDLEY	Ah, good morning, Fusspot. Any letters this morning?
FUSSPOT (Jack Train)	Only one from my wife, sir.
TOMMY HANDLEY	Your wife? Isn't she speaking to you?
FUSSPOT	Oh sir, it's most enjoyable, most enjoyable . . .
TOMMY HANDLEY	What is? Living with Mrs Fusspot? I'd rather eat iron filings.
FUSSPOT	No, it's not that, sir. *(laughs)* She's left me!
TOMMY HANDLEY	Well I'll sleep in my singlet! Left you?
FUSSPOT	*(laughing)* Yes,sir, isn't it awful? She's gone back to London in a huff, sir.
TOMMY HANDLEY	In a huff? Couldn't she get a cab?
FUSSPOT	She says in her letter that you're a — you're a — *(laughs)* —
TOMMY HANDLEY	I'm a what?
FUSSPOT	You're a snake in the grass, sir.
TOMMY HANDLEY	As long as she doesn't say I'm a toad in the hole, I'm all right.
F/X	**TRAMP OF FEET**
TOMMY HANDLEY	Here, get off my desk — you telephone tapper. And take your feet out of my inkwell.

FUSSPOT	She says you're a Jack-in-office, sir, and a . . . .
TOMMY HANDLEY	Puss-in-boots and a pig-in-a-poke.
FUSSPOT	She's a wonderful woman, sir. She's far too good for me.
TOMMY HANDLEY	She frightened the life out of me.
F/X	**CRASH**
TOMMY HANDLEY	Now look what that automatic assassin's done. He's knocked over my aquarium and trod on my tiddlers. Can't you look where you're going?
MAN	Oomph.
TOMMY HANDLEY	I think he's hollow. Well Fusspot, you've got your freedom at last but don't get fresh with the fillies.
FUSSPOT	I'll miss my Tou-Tou, sir — she's far too good for me.
TOMMY HANDLEY	Well don't bring her back here — we've got all the wild animals we want on this farm. Send in Vodkin, will you? I must consider these plans. Now let me see — yes — the cow shed makes a grand studio and what a canteen! Ten times as big as any other room in the building.
F/X	**KNOCK AT DOOR**
TOMMY HANDLEY	Come in!
F/X	**LOUD MOOING OF COWS**
FARMER JOLLOP (Jack Train)	Git on there, Strawberry. Git on Gladys. Eech-oop there, git on . . . .
F/X	**MOOING STILL LOUDER**
TOMMY HANDLEY	Here, take those cows out of my office. Who sent them in here?
JOLLOP	This be only way to pasture now, zur, since they're using cow shed for that danged wireless.
TOMMY HANDLEY	Do you mean to say that every time they're milked they'll come through my office?
JOLLOP	This be only way, zur.
TOMMY HANDLEY	Well I'll be bunkered in the bulrushes! Here am I — the Minister of Aggravation with an office full of cows.

JOLLOP	I'll soon clear 'em out, zur. Ech up Daphne — eel up there.
F/X	**LOUD MOOING UNTIL DOOR CLOSES**
TOMMY HANDLEY	Nice quiet place this.
	(girls whoop in)
CAVENDISH THREE	We're so lonely, Mr Itma — *(singing)*

We ain't nobody's darlings
We are sad as can be
For we ain't got nobody
To make a fuss over we.

TOMMY HANDLEY	Er — well — I'm not doing anything after closing time. Any questions?
CAVENDISH THREE	*(the trio sings an adapted version of 'How D'ya Like to Love Me?' with an occasional response from Tommy until the sequence ends with —)*
	We've asked old Tickle and Jollop to see what they would say, Then when Funf answered We fainted away. How d'ya like to love us and no others —
TOMMY HANDLEY	Where do ye get — these trousers, They your brothers'?
CAVENDISH THREE	How d'ya like your toothbrush a-hanging right alongside ours — How d'ya like it?
TOMMY HANDLEY	I'd rather have a bottle of Persico.
CAVENDISH THREE	Well, all right.
TOMMY HANDLEY	Ah well — a big Government job like this has its compensations. I'm not talking about you, Oomph. Is that phone fixed yet?
MAN	Oomph.
TOMMY HANDLEY	Well go home and phone me up to see if it works, Oomph. I must look over these plans.
F/X	**DOOR OPENS**
VODKIN (Maurice Denham)	Oh, Mr Handemedown. It works, it works!
TOMMY HANDLEY	What does? Our broadcasting station?
VODKIN	No, the egg factory. It has exceeded all my cackle-ations.
TOMMY HANDLEY	Tell me all about it, old cock.
VODKIN	Every hen she lay two times, once in the morning and once at night.
TOMMY HANDLEY	What, no matinées?
VODKIN	At night the hen she sleeps, yes?
TOMMY HANDLEY	Hen-variably.

VODKIN   I switch the light and up she wakes. The cock he crow — the hen she lay. Then again she sleep. Again I switch the light and again she lay. Now a million eggs I have.

TOMMY HANDLEY   I wish I had as many shillings.

VODKIN   What are you going to do?

TOMMY HANDLEY   I know — we'll sell 'em. Call 'em Itma eggs. The yolk of the century. Is our radio station ready?

VODKIN   Oh yes, Mr Hamandegg.

TOMMY HANDLEY   We'll get busy — we'll broadcast the Itma Egg programme right away. Well, folks, the next part of the programme comes to you by courtesy of the Itma Egg Factory — the eggs with chick appeal.

ANNOUNCER (Maurice Denham)   Allo. Ici Radio Twerpenburg. Défense de cracher.

'Ici Radio Twerpenburg, Défense de cracher...'

BAND	**FANFARE**
ANNOUNCER	The Itma All-In Egg Programme.
CAVENDISH THREE	It's those eggs again To put you on your legs again Order 'em now. And do not delay Straight from the cow They are fresh laid today. It's those eggs again The eggs that every grocer hates to sell — So if you feel yeller and want a best smeller Eat Itma and come right out of your shell.
ANNOUNCER	Good evening, everyone. Tonight the makers of Itma eggs — they're oh so strong and ever so shapely — bring you an omelette of 'armony with The Three Cacklers, Scrambled Sam the Double-yoked Yodeller, and Tommy Henlaid — the high cockalorum of comedy — accompanied by Billy Buff-Orpington and his Fowl-Fiddlers.
BAND	**FANFARE**
TOMMY HANDLEY	Hello, yolks — have you ever tried Itma eggs? They're all singing, all humming and all-bumen. The only eggs that are all they're cracked up to be. You'll find the maker's name stamped on the blunt end and countersigned by the rooster on the sharp end. With every dozen we give away a gas mask. Itma eggs can be whipped but they can't be beaten. And now, Scrambled Sam will spread himself on a slice of toast.

Sam Costa	When you've someone you hate in your household
	And you don't know the best thing to do —
	Itma eggs will solve the problem for you.
	Just give him a large one for breakfast
	Or better still, offer him two
	Itma is the egg he'll never pooh-pooh.
	When the egg he starts to crack
	Retire outside the door
	At once the fumes will knock him back
	Unconscious on the floor.
	Drag him out into the open
	And he'll disappear from your view
	Itma eggs have solved your problem for you.

TOMMY HANDLEY Now, folks, here's a charming letter from that well-known provision firm, Grosser Insults Ltd., Coupon Corner. 'Friday. Dear Egg Ma — Itma, Re eggs for regatta. We took the eggs to the party and nobody asked us to stay. So we took them to the local theatre. A baritone was singing "Drake is going west", so we threw some at him but he succeeded in dodging them — are these duck eggs? Yours truly, T. Blender. P.S. When my sugar walks down the street you can have a pound.'
Now, folks, I want you to meet my champion egg layer, Evelyn. Say good Evelyn, Evelyn.

Maurice Denham *(clucks)*

TOMMY HANDLEY How many eggs have you laid today, Evelyn?

Maurice Denham *(more clucks)*

TOMMY HANDLEY Good work. Where were you born, Evelyn?

Maurice Denham *(clucks)*

TOMMY HANDLEY Oh, in an incubator? A self-laid hen, I see? I suppose you haven't always been an egg layer?

Maurice Denham *(clucks)*

TOMMY HANDLEY What were you before you became a hen?

Maurice Denham *(clucks)*

TOMMY HANDLEY Well, fry me on both sides, you've been leading a double life. Tell me, Evelyn, are you married?

Maurice Denham *(indignant noises)*

TOMMY HANDLEY	Oh, I'm so sorry — I see your wedding ring round your left leg. Well, I think you've done extremely well. So, Evelyn, lay off for a week. Well, yolks — eat more Itma Eggs. Itma, Itma, raw, raw, raw.
ANNOUNCER	Mesdames, messieurs, vous pouvez crack 'em. Cock grow.
	(applause)
Maurice Denham	And now Billy Ternent and his syncubators are going to play 'Down the Trail of Dreams' and Denny Dennis sings it.
BAND	**'DOWN THE TRAIL OF DREAMS'**
TOMMY HANDLEY	Now I wonder if that phone's working yet. Hello? Well, I'll flirt in a phone box — no answer. Here, Dotty, I'll finish that jig-saw puzzle. You go down to the village and phone me up.
DOTTY (Vera Lennox)	Okay, Mr Handmaid. Can Mr Fusspot go with me?
TOMMY HANDLEY	What's that? I thought Fusspot was your bête noir, whatever that means.
DOTTY	Oh, he's been ever so nice since his wife went away. He says I'm his dream girl and his little lump of liquorice.
TOMMY HANDLEY	The perishing old pontefract cake.
DOTTY	And he says I wake the gypsy in his soul.
TOMMY HANDLEY	Well cross my palm with butter.
DOTTY	Yes, and he says he never knew what love meant till he met me.
TOMMY HANDLEY	And him with fourteen little Fusspots. I'll have to stop this. I'll hide his teeth, that's what I'll do. Send him in.
DOTTY	Don't be hard on him, Mr Hambone.
TOMMY HANDLEY	I'll deal with him. I know how to cure these men when they're between the norty forties and the nifty fifties. Now I must go and see how the Itma radio station's getting on. Well — I'll plant a pansy in the pig sty. Will you look at Mrs Tickle! Riding breeches and a bowler hat. Here, Tickle, what's all this?
MRS TICKLE (Maurice Denham)	Oh, Mr Itma — I've been taking riding lessons.
TOMMY HANDLEY	I can't have my charwoman strutting round here in jodhpurs.

MRS TICKLE	But Mr Jollop says he's going to take me to the 'Unt.
TOMMY HANDLEY	The 'Unt? Why, if the hounds see you there won't half be a tantivy. You get off your G.G. and make me a cup of T.T.
MRS TICKLE	Yoicks, Mr Itma. Tally ho.
TOMMY HANDLEY	And tally candle to you.
F/X	**DOOR SLAMS**
MRS TICKLE	Oh dear, he's left me all alone. I don't know what I shall do if that Mr Funf should phone.
F/X	**KNOCK AT DOOR**
MRS TICKLE	Come in. Oh, it's you, Mr Jollop.
JOLLOP	Aye — me it be. I saw Old Itma go out and so I said 'Jarge', I said, 'now's your chance to get that girt big kiss you've been waiting for.'
MRS TICKLE	Oh, Mr Jollop, you're a regular John Doings, that's what you are.
JOLLOP	Come on now, give oi a real walloper.
MRS TICKLE	Oh, give over, Mr Jollop — and me in my breeches.
JOLLOP	You look very pretty in them.
	(general scuffle)
MRS TICKLE	Mr Jollop — you mustn't.
JOLLOP	Eee — I bin to pictures last noight, and I see how it's done — chap there he grabs lass like this . . . .
MRS TICKLE	Ooh, you he-man!

F/X	**DOOR OPENS**
TOMMY HANDLEY	What's that — the 'Unt? Nice goings on in a Government Office, I must say. Lola, I'll lock you in the larder if I have any more of this. And as for you, Jollop, back to the barnyard. Did you ever see such a Disorderly Room.
F/X	**DOOR SLAMS**
TOMMY HANDLEY	I wonder if there have been any phone calls. *(picks up phone)* Hello, is anybody there? No? *(replaces receiver)* Not a nibble.
F/X	**DOOR OPENS**
TOMMY HANDLEY	Ah, Fusspot — you're just the man I want. We've got to get more publicity for Itma — start a big campaign.
FUSSPOT	Not a moment too soon, sir. There have been more questions in Parliament about you, sir.
TOMMY HANDLEY	There'll be questions in the Police Gazette about you soon.
FUSSPOT	Me, sir?
TOMMY HANDLEY	Yes, for making passes at my secretary. I've heard of your amorous advances.
FUSSPOT	It's the tiger in me, sir. I always break out in the spring.
TOMMY HANDLEY	You'd better try Persico. I know that in the spring a young man's fancy — I mean a young fiancée — it isn't spring anyhow — it's winter.
FUSSPOT	Ah, sir, when winter comes . . . .
TOMMY HANDLEY	You wilt in your woollies. Now keep your mind on your memos. The first shot in my publicity campaign will be on the air — tonight. So get busy.
F/X	**DOOR OPENS**
TOMMY HANDLEY	What is it, Vodkin?
VODKIN	All is ready, sir. Your radio station — she will wipe the noise of the BBC right off the air. I put this loud spikker on your desk, so. Then you will hear sitting at your desk.
TOMMY HANDLEY	I can't stand sitting at my desk. I'd rather bend down and listen at my leisure. Right, Vodkin. We'll be on the air in three minutes. Itma will tell the world.
F/X	**TELEPHONE RINGS**

This is Funf speaking—

TOMMY HANDLEY	Well, dab my dial with distemper. It's working at last. Is that you Dotty?
FUNF (Jack Train)	No, I am not Dotty. This is Funf speaking.
TOMMY HANDLEY	Funf? How did you know I was on the phone?
FUNF	Because it was I – Funf – who fixed the phone in your office.
TOMMY HANDLEY	You were in my office?
FUNF	Yes, and I have the plans of your radio station.
TOMMY HANDLEY	So you were Oomph.
FUNF	Yes, Funf was Oomph.
TOMMY HANDLEY	Well, I'll cough up all the coppers in the cash box.
FUNF	Now at last you will experience my Merry Designs.
TOMMY HANDLEY	I'm not frightened of you, Funf. I'll see you next Tuesday.
FUNF	No, not Tuesday – Friday.

TOMMY HANDLEY	Friday?
FUNF	Yes, Friday.
TOMMY HANDLEY	Friday.
FUNF	Friday.
BOTH	FRIDAY.
	(applause)
ANNOUNCER	Once more Funf has foiled The Minister of Aggravation and Mysteries. Itma is temporarily incapacitated by the shock, so I'll get the band to revive him with 'Somewhere in France', with Sam Costa.
SAM COSTA & BAND	'SOMEWHERE IN FRANCE'. SEGUE INTO SIGNATURE TUNE
F/X	BUZZER
TOMMY HANDLEY	Now for the opening of the Itma Publicity Campaign. I never felt so nervous in my life. I'll be on the air in a minute — I'll just try a few words into the mike, as I believe they call it. Then Vodkin can carry on. I have to start as soon as the purple light shows. There it is — no, it's Vodkin's nose. *(sings)* When the deep purple light makes me split my sleeves with fright . . . . . Good gasworks — I'm on the air. Good evening, Great Britain. As Minister of Aggravation it is my duty tonight on the umpteenth day of the war against Depression to explain to you that I have seven hundred further restrictions to impose upon you. Here in the heart of the country I have been able to think out some of the most irritating regulations you've ever heard of, but first of all I have tried them out on the home front — on my staff and on the other animals on my farm — so now you'll hear what they think of them. Tell me, Mr Fusspot, what do you think of my wife-restriction rule?
FUSSPOT	Oh, sir, it's most intriguing — most rejuvenating.
TOMMY HANDLEY	I thought you'd say that, you flannel-footed old philanderer. And what's your opinion, Mrs Tickle, of my rule regarding shorter shirts for scarecrows?
MRS TICKLE	Well, sir, I always does my best for all my gentlemen.
TOMMY HANDLEY	You shirty old sud-splasher. Now, Dotty, are you in favour of my latest idea — coupon for kisses?
DOTTY	Oh yes, Mr Handsqueeze — I've used up four books already.
TOMMY HANDLEY	The lips that touch kippers can never touch mine. And you, Jollop — are you in favour of the prohibition of bath water?

JOLLOP	That I am, sir — though how it 'elps me I don't rightly know. I haven't had a bath since Jubilee.
TOMMY HANDLEY	We'll have you de-contaminated. Finally, folks, I'll ask my animals what they think of the great Itma. Mrs Cow, forward — what is your opinion of the great Itma?
COW (Maurice Denham)	Itma, Itma, moo moo moo.
TOMMY HANDLEY	Thanks, I'll shake you by the crumpled for that. Now, Mrs Porker.
PIG (Maurice Denham)	Good old Itma. I wish I had as many chitterlings.
TOMMY HANDLEY	Splendid. Let me grip your trotter and my dear Mrs Duck — you ought to know your proper gander.
DUCK (Maurice Denham)	Quack, Itma, etc.
TOMMY HANDLEY	Excellent. The compliments of the seasoning to you. And last but not least — one of my hybrid animals which I obtained by crossing a pig with a sheep . . . . .
VOICE (Jack Train)	I think it's positively Persico.
TOMMY HANDLEY	What's that? Whose voice is that?
FUNF	This is Funf speaking. I, too, have a secret radio.
TOMMY HANDLEY	Well, I'll be tickled with a turnip.
	(applause)
BAND	**SIGNATURE TUNE TO FINISH**

The ITMA series which had shared its beginnings with the war ended in February 1940. Though the O.O.T. had already been removed to the country, it was decided to evacuate its members once again: in the last programme their rural haven was taken over by the Army and the residents were sent off in caravans to find a new home, with Funf in hot pursuit. When the series next came on the air—nearly a year and a half later—the BBC Variety Department had itself been evacuated for the second time, to Bangor. The intervening months had seen the end of the 'phoney war' and the beginning of the German drive through Western Europe. The Low Countries had fallen, France was occupied, and Britain was under severe attack from the air. By the summer of 1941 the country was fully engaged in its fight for survival.

It was in this atmosphere that the second series of ITMA began. Take-offs on Government ministries, however good-natured, would no longer be well-received and it was felt that Handley's weekly antics should provide more of an escape for war-weary listeners and, perhaps, a touch of nostalgia. The public was being urged to have its holidays at home rather than the traditional fortnight at the sea, so the ITMA team opted to provide the missing pleasures of the seaside. The summer series took place at Foaming-at-the-Mouth, the epitome of all that was shabby and inefficient in a small resort, with Tommy standing for, and then elected to, the office of Mayor. The name of the series was changed to ITSA—'It's That Sand Again!'

Of the original cast, only Vera Lennox and Jack Train were left; after touring in Jack Hylton's production of a stage version of ITMA through the spring of 1940, Maurice Denham and Sam Costa had been called up. New members were drawn from the Variety Rep, now all in Bangor, and included Horace Percival, Sydney Keith, Clarence Wright, Dorothy Summers, and Fred Yule. Music was provided by the BBC Variety Orchestra, conducted by Charles Shadwell. With this enlarged cast, and the popularity of the previous series still fresh in their minds, the scope seemed limitless as producer, writer, and comic met to discuss the first programme. The relative failure of the stage version had underlined the fact that radio was the only medium suitable to—and fully exploited by—the ITMA style, and it was this summer series which produced a fusion of the elements which would be ITMA for the next seven years: a basic, if slim, storyline, sustained by an endless procession of crazy characters through the overworked door—often for no particular reason—each of whom introduced himself with the requisite catchphrase. Although he was the central figure, there was no strict division of comic and feed between Handley and this calvacade; roles were interchangeable and laughs evenly distributed. The only demand made by an affectionate public was that all the characters should appear and, weekly, deliver the lines for which they were loved.

Some of the best-known ITMA figures date from this period: Sam Scram (Sydney Keith), Handley's American henchman; Ali Oop (Horace Percival), eternal vendor of saucy postcards; Clarence Wright's chirpy commercial traveller, never making a sale but never seeming to care; Claude and Cecil (Percival and Train), rendered practically useless by their exaggerated deference to one another—'After you, Claude. No—after *you*, Cecil.'—and so on. Perhaps the most poignant character was the Diver (Horace Percival) who stood by the dingy seaside plaintively reminding all who passed to remember him and who regularly announced that he was 'going down now, sir'.

ITMA was a cosy, personal programme, and it was this familiarity that provided comfort during the war. The catchphrases gave the public something to hold on to in a distinctly threatening atmosphere. Their psychological importance was demonstrated daily: sometimes the last words spoken by a bomber pilot preparing for his descent were 'I'm going down now, sir'.

The summer series ended in July, and was soon followed by another which began in September. Tommy Handley returned to office as His Washout the Mayor of Foaming-at-the-Mouth, accompanied by his new foreign secretary, Signor So-So (Dino Galvani). So-So had been intended as an Italian version of Funf but his chronic mismanagement of the English tongue proved too endearing and he remained at Handley's side as a well-loved language joke. ('Ah, you attract me like a maggot,' he once remarked to one of the ladies. 'Let me cuss you on both cheeks.')

This series, which had returned to the proper title of ITMA, produced one of the immortals in the history of radio characterization: Mrs Mopp the Corporation Cleanser (Dorothy Summers) sent by 'the Labour' to dust the Mayor's dado. Introduced in October, she became the classic cockney char. Entering with the slightly gravelly, and certainly forceful, 'Can I do you now, sir?', her dialogue peppered with *double entendres*, she made a weekly ritual of presenting His Washup with a small gift. Her exit line of 'Ta-ta for now' would later be shortened to the famous T.T.F.N. Like many of the other ITMA characters, Mrs Mopp provided a catchphrase which occasionally transcended itself when repeated in the context of a war-torn country: hearing a warden pass by, a small boy in Bath who was trapped under the rubble of what had once been a home called out 'Can you do me now, sir?', and T.T.F.N. was sometimes the last intelligible phrase uttered by people who were dying in hospital.

Clarence Wright

Alias
Commercial Traveller
Man From The Ministry

Remembers

'Memory brings the light of other days'

It was always fun to be with Tommy Handley. I had the tremendous pleasure and the privilege of appearing with him at most of his public and private stage and cabaret performances during the last seven years of his life.

Tommy was highly inventive with his gags and pranks, original, very funny, but never unkind. However, his thoughts were constantly on the next ITMA. The next programme had to be better than the last. It was a positive mental strain for him. He was an unselfish performer, always helpful to the other characters, especially kind to new members of the cast. Whilst he was That Man he was elated at other artistes' success in obtaining laughs.

For a number of years we appeared together in 'Tommy Handley's Half Hour', which was broadcast live from the Criterion Theatre, Piccadilly, London, every Tuesday at 1.00 p.m. This show, like ITMA, was simultaneously recorded and later transmitted throughout the world. Only once did I say to him 'We cannot crack this gag, Tommy,' and he asked, 'Why not?' I said, 'It's old,' and he replied, 'Surely it's the way we deliver the line.' Came the show, it was a situation sketch, I 'fed' him into his line, he delivered it—it was a yell. The laugh lasted long enough for him to whisper 'Was that all right?' He made it seem as if he had just thought of it. A radio comic genius.

Once, in ITMA, the effects men—who were always kept busy—missed the door for my entrance. We could not have a pause, so I came in and began my lines. He said, 'Wait a minute, how did you get here? You must have slipped under the door.'

Travelling in a train from an engagement, the windows were steamed up and there had been no conversation among the occupants, Tommy leaned forward to the passenger sitting opposite in a window seat and said, 'Excuse me, sir. Have we passed "Tadpolium" yet?' The man wiped the window with his newspaper and replied, 'Yes, I think so.' Tom said 'Thank you' and continued to read his paper.

Once he told me that the previous evening he had seen a splendid film. He was queuing for the advertised feature when he noticed a number of his friends, cinema critics, arriving by taxi and entering the cinema. He knew that this particular movie house was used to try out new films on an unsuspecting public, to gauge their box office potential from the audience reaction. He left his place in the queue, walked to the vestibule, and quickly said to the commissionaire 'Persico and Merry Designs'. The commissionaire said, 'Yes sir, up the stairs, centre gangway.' He told me he was dying to go back and ask the commissionaire what he thought he had said, but on second thought decided not to do so as he might have been thrown out. A very modest man.

Recently, when I was talking to a now well-known composer, he told me that once, during the war, it happened that he was leaving our Club at the same time as Tommy. He knew Tommy as a member and they had spoken together only a little. Tommy said, 'I'm walking up Regent Street. Are you going that way?' The musician said he could—he had no appointments and enjoyed the chatter as they walked. When they arrived at a well-known outfitters, Tommy said, 'I want to go in and buy an overcoat.' Tommy tried on a few and then turned to our friend and said, 'This would suit you, try it on,' which he did. Tommy told him to keep it on and in a manner which avoided any embarrassment explained that he, Tommy, was lucky and in work. There being no work for the man's type of composing at the time, how could he, through circumstance, buy a new coat? (The musician's own coat was old and worn.) To my knowledge, Tommy never mentioned this to a soul.

Each week on Thursday, from the time he left his native Liverpool, he wrote a long letter to his mother and enclosed cash in the registered envelope. We played concerts in and around Liverpool about three times each year. We both stayed in his mother's house and Tommy always brought thoughtful gifts which gave her obvious happiness. He truly was 'Mrs Handley's boy, her pride and joy'.

When the ITMA door closed for the last time, Tommy left many happy and pleasant memories and, thank heavens, a number of recordings.

Clarence Wright

With the rigours of food rationing (*bottom right*), constant bomb damage (*bottom left*), and bedding down in Underground stations (*middle right*) or air raid shelters, ITMA was a welcome break each week. *Left*, Jack Train and Horace Percival as Claude and Cecil; *middle left*, Handley threatens to clip a few of Charles Shadwell's hairs.

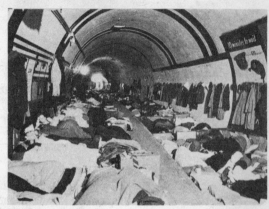

Tommy Handley
in
It's That Man Again

(No. 28 Fourth series—No. 59)
Transmission
Friday, 3rd April 1942, 8.30-9.00 p.m.
Home Service
Sunday, 5th April 1942, 9.30-10.00 a.m.
Forces

ANNOUNCER	Ladies and gentlemen — Tommy Handley! Yes — 'It's That Man Again!'
ORCHESTRA	SIGNATURE TUNE
OMNES	It's that man again, Yes, that man again, Yes sir, Tommy Handley is here!
ANNOUNCER	With the courage of his many convictions our musical Mayor intends to build in this borough a full symphony orchestra conducted by —
OMNES	Mother's pride and joy Mrs Handley's boy, Oh, it's useless to complain — When trouble's brewing, it's his doing, That man, that man again!
SIGNOR SO—SO (Dino Galvani)	Pray violins for his Bandstand the Mayor!

(applause)

TOMMY HANDLEY	Don't applaud now — wait until you hear my new Foaming Symphony Orchestra. We used to have one here before the war, but many of the players left the orchestra to join the Army — now the Army wants to join the orchestra. Our Friday night free and easy concerts were a colossal success. For fourpence you could get a catalogue, a cantata, a cream cornet and a cold if you sat near the trombone. We played all the classics — The Charge of the Laundry by Liszt, Beethoven's Too Ripe Tomato, Elgar's Circumpump and Stance, Offenbach's Horses and Knees Up Mother Brahms. Nobody ever stayed after the first bar — they made for the nearest one. This time we'll lock the door and fasten it with an Adrian Boult. Ah, the Bliss of hearing good music!

F/X	**PHONE**
TOMMY HANDLEY	Hello?
HARI KARI (Jack Train)	*(jabber)*
TOMMY HANDLEY	Yes, we've got a double one.
HARI KARI	*(jabber)*
TOMMY HANDLEY	There's room for two.
HARI KARI	*(jabber)*
TOMMY HANDLEY	Of course you can lock the door.
F/X	**PHONE RINGS OFF**
TOMMY HANDLEY	That was Hitched Up — he wants to book a room in the Corporation hostel. Now I must pacify my Municipal Bandmaster. He won't like being augmented.
F/X	**DOOR OPENS**
COMMERCIAL TRAVELLER (Clarence Wright)	Good morning!
TOMMY HANDLEY	Good morning.
TRAVELLER	*Nice* day!
TOMMY HANDLEY	Very.
TRAVELLER	I'm disposing of all my surplus stock — bargains in every department. Any offers?
TOMMY HANDLEY	No.
TRAVELLER	Thank you. I hope you'll extend your patronage to my successor?
TOMMY HANDLEY	Are you leaving me?
TRAVELLER	Yes — I've been called up. Good morning!
TOMMY HANDLEY	Sad morning.
TRAVELLER	Lacka-day!

F/X	**DOOR CLOSES**
TOMMY HANDLEY	That was Reggie Stration. Before I have any more interruptions, I'll make out today's programme. 9.30 a.m.: Rise with the lark. 9.35: Let lark out of window. 10.00 a.m.: Ring for swallow — enter landlady. Not my pigeon. 10.30: Turn on wireless. 10.35: Turn on side. 11 o'clock: Turn up trumps. 12 noon: Get up regardless. 1.00 p.m.: Attend audition for extra musicians — jew's harp, triangle, mouth organ and mangle. 1.5: Book 'em all. 1.10: Sack 'em all. 9.40: Welcome 'All.
F/X	**DOOR OPENS**
COMMERCIAL TRAVELLER (Paula Green)	Good morning!
TOMMY HANDLEY	Good gracious.
TRAVELLER	*Nice* day.
TOMMY HANDLEY	Delightful.
TRAVELLER	Any tonics, tinctures or pick-me-ups?
TOMMY HANDLEY	No.
TRAVELLER	Thank you. I'll call again.
TOMMY HANDLEY	Good morning.
TRAVELLER	*Nice* day.
F/X	**DOOR CLOSES**
TOMMY HANDLEY	That was Sal Volatile — she's taken the place of that awful bore, Assick. I hope she does call again.
F/X	**DOOR OPENS**
TRAVELLER	I will.
F/X	**DOOR CLOSES**
TOMMY HANDLEY	Nice girl. It's time these musicians arrived for their auditions. I'd better take the cotton wool out of my musical ear — that's the one I play the piano by.
F/X	**PHONE, THEN DOOR OPENS**

SIGNOR SO–SO	Scusi — I answer that.
TOMMY HANDLEY	All right. Put your ear to the official receiver.
SO–SO	Hello? Oh, too bad. Too bad.
TOMMY HANDLEY	He's been buying eggs.
SO–SO	No . . . no.
TOMMY HANDLEY	Yes, yes.
SO–SO	Oh, I couldn't do that.
TOMMY HANDLEY	Go on — risk it.
SO–SO	But it is impossible.
TOMMY HANDLEY	Get away, So-So! Give the girl her money.
SO–SO	You are nothing less than a black molar.
TOMMY HANDLEY	He's talking to a shady dentist.
SO–SO	With you I have no more to do — I kiss you goodbye.
TOMMY HANDLEY	I'll ask you for tuppence.
F/X	**PHONE RINGS OFF**
TOMMY HANDLEY	What was all that about?
SO–SO	Notting at all, notting at all.
TOMMY HANDLEY	You have been talking to your better self. Go and see if my extra musicians have arrived, will you? You'll know them — their coats say 'goodnight' and their trousers say 'good morning'.
F/X	**DOOR CLOSES**
TOMMY HANDLEY	I wonder where I'll put this Symphony Orchestra. I can't use the bandstand — all our old sea-dogs are using it as a kennel.
F/X	**DOOR OPENS**
TOMMY HANDLEY	Well, if it isn't Mrs Mopp, the char with the bald-headed broom.
MRS MOPP (Dorothy Summers)	Can I do you now sir?

TOMMY HANDLEY	Yes, Mrs Mopp. I want you to pacify my landlady, Cheap Chat.
MRS MOPP	Her, sir? I wouldn't lower me dignity by talking to her. She's a woman, that's what she is — a woman!
TOMMY HANDLEY	You confirm my worst suspicions.
MRS MOPP	What I could tell you about her and her daughter!
TOMMY HANDLEY	Some other time, Mrs Mopp. What about her daughter? Anyway, she threatens me with expulsion.
MRS MOPP	How dare she! You've never had it, have you, sir?
TOMMY HANDLEY	No — I've had brewers' asthma and a touch of the tantivies, but never expulsion.
MRS MOPP	I could let you have a nice combined room, sir. It may not be clean, but it's comfortable. My present lodger's been pinched again.
TOMMY HANDLEY	What — between the mattress and the ironwork? I'll think it over. I should be very happy in Maison Mopp.
MRS MOPP	I'll get rid of the pigeons before you move in. Ta-ta for now.
TOMMY HANDLEY	Hotpot for stew.
F/X	**DOOR CLOSES**
TOMMY HANDLEY	Now wasn't that nice of her. I think I'll start my mopping up operations right away.
F/X	**DOOR OPENS**
ALI OOP (Horace Percival)	Excuse please.
TOMMY HANDLEY	Why, it's aroma of the South Seas. What do you want?
ALI OOP	Your police try to stop me peddling on steps of Town Hall.
TOMMY HANDLEY	You certainly choose some very public places.
ALI OOP	In other towns I peddle where I please.
TOMMY HANDLEY	Ah, but we're very particular here.
ALI OOP	You give me licence — I give you very funny toy. Make loud noises when sat on.

TOMMY HANDLEY	They used to laugh when I sat down at the piano. You get out of here and take your penetrating effluvia with you.
ALI OOP	I go — I come back.

F/X	**DOOR CLOSES**
TOMMY HANDLEY	Now, before I decide on how many musicians I need to turn my Town Band into a Symphony Orchestra, I'd better interview my bandmaster.
F/X	**BUZZER**
TOMMY HANDLEY	Send him in, will you?
F/X	**DOOR OPENS**
Charles Shadwell	You sent for me, Your Tomship?
TOMMY HANDLEY	Yes, Your Tuneup. Have you ever conducted a Symphony Orchestra?
Charles Shadwell	Of course I have. Once I was known as the Great Shadwelloffski.
TOMMY HANDLEY	When did you cut off your Offski?
Charles Shadwell	When I was naturalised.
TOMMY HANDLEY	B naturalised, I suppose. I'm thinking of having you augmented. What's your new affront to the public today?

Charles Shadwell	The 'Camptown Races' arranged by Clive Richardson.
TOMMY HANDLEY	I thought it was arranged by Bob-tailed Nag.
ORCHESTRA	'CAMPTOWN RACES'
	(applause)
TOMMY HANDLEY	I thought that was going to run all night. It's a grand day for the Race.
Charles Shadwell	What Race?
TOMMY HANDLEY	The Human Race.
Charles Shadwell	How would you know?
TOMMY HANDLEY	What programme is this — ITMA or Hi Gang?
Charles Shadwell	I'll go and find out.
TOMMY HANDLEY	Do.
Charles Shadwell	Good morning — *nice* day.
F/X	**DOOR CLOSES**

TOMMY HANDLEY	I'll have to sack that man — he's getting too big for his baton. Now Easter's nearly with us I must line up some attractions. I think I'll have a cattle show in the Town Hall, a guest night in the Henry Hall, and I'll write to my sister in Montreal.
F/X	DOOR OPENS
SIGNOR SO–SO	Mr Handicap — one of your musicians has come. He is a big-pipe player.
TOMMY HANDLEY	A big-pipe player? You mean an organist.
SO–SO	Oh no, I mean the blow-pipes. He is a Scotcher.
TOMMY HANDLEY	A Scotcher? Oh, I've got you — he's a Highlander.
SO–SO	No, not an Irelander. He comes from Scotland with his big pipes. He wears a klit.
TOMMY HANDLEY	A klit?
SO–SO	Oh yes, a Scottish klit —
TOMMY HANDLEY	You mean a kilt?
SO–SO	That's what I said — a klit.
TOMMY HANDLEY	Listen So-So — a K–I–L–T — klit.
SO–SO	You mean *kilt*. It is like the ladies wear. It is like a squirt.
TOMMY HANDLEY	Ladies don't wear squirts, they marry them. I can't see him now, So-So. Make him play outside the lighthouse to frighten the seagulls away.
F/X	DOOR CLOSES
TOMMY HANDLEY	This'll be a sensation — a piper in a symphony orchestra. Now I only want a piano accordion and an ocharina and the combination is complete.
F/X	DOOR OPENS
BOOKHAM (Jack Train)	Good morning. Good morning.
TOMMY HANDLEY	Ah, Mr Bookham. The agent with the Charing Cross eyes!
BOOKHAM	Mr Mayor, I've had the rudest shock of my life. Last Friday —
TOMMY HANDLEY	Tell the kids I never said it.

BOOKHAM	No. I got the shock when I heard you were bringing a symp-hony orchestra down here for Easter. There's no money in symp-hony orchestras Mr Mayor, not a sausage.
TOMMY HANDLEY	Nobody's going to play a sausage in my orchestra.
BOOKHAM	The moment I heard of your Easter arrangements I said to myself wo-ho!
TOMMY HANDLEY	Not ha-ha.
BOOKHAM	No-ho!
TOMMY HANDLEY	Just wo-ho?
BOOKHAM	Yes, Mr Mayor — wo-ho! I said the Mayor must have a funfair, like Dreamland at Margate or the pleasure beach at Blackpool.
TOMMY HANDLEY	Now you're talking.
BOOKHAM	I looked round your place this morning and the moment I saw the lighthouse I said to myself —
TOMMY HANDLEY	That's a lighthouse.
BOOKHAM	I can make it into a helter-skelter. I can book all the biggest attractions in Britain — the fattest woman in the world, the Wall of Death, the Whoopee Water Chute!
F/X	**RATTLE OF COINS IN BOX**
TOMMY HANDLEY	What's that?
F/X	**MORE RATTLE**
BOOKHAM	Sounds like money to me. As soon as I heard that jingle I said to myself —
THE DIVER (Horace Percival)	Don't forget the diver, sir. Don't forget the diver.
TOMMY HANDLEY	I never give to dry divers. What's the idea of rattling that empty money box?
THE DIVER	Every penny makes the water warmer, sir. Every penny makes the water warmer.
TOMMY HANDLEY	Here's a bob's worth — now simmer off.
F/X	**MONEY INTO BOX**
THE DIVER	*(going off)* Don't forget the diver, sir — every penny makes the water warmer.

TOMMY HANDLEY	Bookham — I'll do it. Off with the symphony concerts — on with the funfair. Get busy right away. Send in my two assistants as you go out, will you?
BOOKHAM	I thought you'd like it. As soon as I got the notion I said to myself —
BOTH	Wo-ho!
TOMMY HANDLEY	Off you go-ho, and don't sla-ham the do-hor.
F/X	**DOUBLE DOOR SLAM**
TOMMY HANDLEY	This is much more in my line. Concerts bore me stiff, but a funfair — wo-ho!
F/X	**DOOR OPENS**

CECIL (Horace Percival)	After you, Claude —
CLAUDE (Jack Train)	No — after *you*, Cecil!
TOMMY HANDLEY	Cut out the etiquette — you've a big job to do.

CECIL	Do you want us to push your chair, Mr Mayor?
CLAUDE	It'll need a new tyre, sire.
TOMMY HANDLEY	No. I want you to go round to the lighthouse and lend a hand erecting our Foaming Fun Fair.
CECIL	Will there be swings and things?
CLAUDE	There'll be coconut shies I surmise.
TOMMY HANDLEY	Yes, and merry-go-rounds, you hounds.
CECIL	There'll be side-shows, Mose —
CLAUDE	Aye, and fan-dancers, Francis.
TOMMY HANDLEY	You'll see many a worse 'un Sandy Macpherson.
CECIL	Then we'll have a dekko Sir Echo.
CLAUDE	We'll have a penn'orth Sir Kenneth.
TOMMY HANDLEY	Yes, you'll get a shock Sir Cock — now away you go.
CECIL	After you, Pig —
CLAUDE	No — after *you*, Whistle.
F/X	**DOOR CLOSES**
TOMMY HANDLEY	There's one thing I've forgotten. I must convene a meeting of the Council.
F/X	**BUZZER**
TOMMY HANDLEY	Hello? Is that the Town Clerk?
TOWN CLERK (Jack Train)	Yes. Are you ther Mr Mer?
TOMMY HANDLEY	Yes, I'm on tap old chap. Call a meeting of the Council right away, will you?
TOWN CLERK	The Council is sitting now. I'm in the cher.
TOMMY HANDLEY	Who put you ther?
TOWN CLERK	It's me they prefer.

TOMMY HANDLEY	Well, I'm coming round at once — I'll run like a her. This is a nice thing — a meeting of the Corporation and I'm not awer. They'd better have a ker. Band — play me to the Town Hall.
ORCHESTRA	MUSIC LINK
TOMMY HANDLEY	All part of the Itma service. I'd better go in and face them.
F/X	DOOR OPENS
	(uproar)
Fred Yule	Pray silence for his Lateship the Mayor.
	(renewed uproar)
TOWN CLERK	I shall now evacuate the cher, Mr Mer.
TOMMY HANDLEY	Thank you Town Clerk, you old nark. Now gentlemen —
Fred Yule	What's all this about a ten-penny orchestra?
TOMMY HANDLEY	That's all off.
Sydney Keith	*(old)* I've heard him —
TOMMY HANDLEY	Heard who?
Sydney Keith	Victor Orloff — he's got a sextette.
TOMMY HANDLEY	Keep sex out of this. The Symphony Orchestra's fallen through.
Fred Yule	Fallen through what?
VOICE	Fallen through what?
TOMMY HANDLEY	No fault of their own. Councillor Cheese-cake, I'm surprised at you.
Dorothy Summers	We're all surprised at you. You're not a Mayor, you're a monster.
TOMMY HANDLEY	You must have seen my Lochness in the paper. The proposition I put before you today concerns a funfair to be held in and around the Lighthouse.
Fred Yule	A funfair — it's preposterous.
TOMMY HANDLEY	It isn't — it's Easter.
F/X	PHONE
TOMMY HANDLEY	Hullo?

FUNF (Jack Train)	This is Funf speaking.
F/X	**MACHINE GUN**
TOMMY HANDLEY	Missed him. Now gentlemen, I will proceed with the business of the day.
VOICE	Your lunch, sir.
TOMMY HANDLEY	Thanks.
F/X	**POP, THEN DRINKING SOUND**
TOMMY HANDLEY	What's for afters?
VOICE	This, sir.
TOMMY HANDLEY	Oh, thanks.
F/X	**POP, THEN DRINKING SOUND**
TOMMY HANDLEY	Swallowed unanimously. Having disposed of that, the moment has now come when I —
Horace Percival	Shave, sir?
TOMMY HANDLEY	Thank you. Why it's Dan Druff my barber. Come in, Dan.
F/X	**STROPPING NOISES**
TOMMY HANDLEY	Now gentlemen — start the shave, Dan — with your approval this is what I propose to do.
F/X	**LATHERING NOISES**
TOMMY HANDLEY	I — er — *(coughs)* — that's rather nice shaving soap that, Dan . . . Make it vanilla next time. I propose to —
Horace Percival	Lift your chin, sir.
TOMMY HANDLEY	Oh, right.
F/X	**SANDPAPER NOISES**
TOMMY HANDLEY	I propose to —
Horace Percival	What's the razor like?
TOMMY HANDLEY	Razor? I thought it was a broken bottle — ooh . . .

VOICE	Mr Mayor, what are you trying to do?
TOMMY HANDLEY	Stick my chin on again. Now, will the Corporation vote the necessary funds?
OMNES	No.
TOMMY HANDLEY	Carried unanimously.
	(uproar)
TOMMY HANDLEY	That concludes the business for today. I'll draw the necessary funds from the City Treasurer.
Clarence Wright	You'll be in hot water if you do *(maniacal laugh)*.
TOMMY HANDLEY	Hot water? Why not. Every penny makes the water warmer.
	(more protests as Councillors exit)
F/X	DOOR CLOSES
TOMMY HANDLEY	The Council takes things too seriously. I could understand it if I was using their soap. Come on Sam, let's go down to the canteen and have my shoes soled with stewed steak.
F/X	DOOR OPENS
Kay Cavendish & Paula Green	Hullo, Mr Mayor.
TOMMY HANDLEY	Why, it's my Beauty Queens — you're just in time to fasten my collar at the back.
Paula Green	We've got a song for Your Cut-throat.
TOMMY HANDLEY	That's fine — what is it?
Kay Cavendish	The Lollipop Man.
TOMMY HANDLEY	Well, sing it while I plaster my face up.
KAY CAVENDISH, PAULA GREEN & ORCHESTRA	'THE LOLLIPOP MAN'
	(applause)
F/X	DOOR OPENS

SAM SCRAM	Boss! Boss! I bin looking for you everywhere. Your new film's all ready.
TOMMY HANDLEY	What — the one I made about my theatrical career?
SAM	Sure boss. It's the most terrific third-rate, twice nightly, touring tear-up ever tried out by our tintinabulating thespians, theatrically titivated, on this or any other terrestrial territory.
TOMMY HANDLEY	You're a big tease — that's what you are. Meeting adjoined again. You can all come and see it — come in on your passes and go out on your elbows.
ORCHESTRA	'TOM MARCHES ON', THEN SHORT FANFARE
Jack Train	Stage-struck Films Incorporated present an all-tumbling, all mumbling, all flumbling film epic photographed in glorious ringside colour entitled —
ORCHESTRA	LONG FANFARE UP AND UNDER
Jack Train	'Tom Tells the Tale!'
ORCHESTRA	FANFARE UP AND OUT
Horace Percival	Tonight His Spotlight the Mayor takes the stage to describe to you in a fabricated farago of fictitious fragments his theatrical career which he has called 'From Ring to Ruin' or 'From Circus to Workhus'.
TOMMY HANDLEY	Start up the projector, Hector.
F/X	PROJECTOR SOUNDS
TOMMY HANDLEY	Like many another famous star of stage and screen radio, I was —
Fred Yule	Who was?
TOMMY HANDLEY	I was.
Fred Yule	You was?
TOMMY HANDLEY	Yus. As I was about to say, I come of theatrical stock, my parents being respectively chief chucker out at the Coliseum, Cowdenbeath and assistant wardrobe mistress at the Palladium, Pwlleli. Here you see —
Fred Yule	There's nothing on the screen.
TOMMY HANDLEY	Don't be in a hurry — I'm not born yet. My father became, eventually, a great Empire builder. You will find his far-flung Empires . . .
OMNES	(sing) All over the place.

TOMMY HANDLEY	Yes. At Walton-on-Taze, Wart-on-Nose, and Bunion-on-Back.
Horace Percival	Is this a film or an organ recital?
TOMMY HANDLEY	Change the slide, Sam. My early years were spent in theatrical baskets.
Clarence Wright	Looking for gags.
TOMMY HANDLEY	If I had one I'd use it on you.
Clarence Wright	You couldn't, you used it last week.
TOMMY HANDLEY	Well, this is a series, isn't it? To continue. At the early age of seven I joined a travelling circus and learned the equestrian arts. I rode one horse twice nightly and two horses once nightly.
VOICE	What about matinées?
TOMMY HANDLEY	They wouldn't pay me extra so I rode my high horse.
Fred Yule	Who did?
TOMMY HANDLEY	I did.
Fred Yule	You did?
TOMMY HANDLEY	Yus. I also practised on the slack wire.
SIGNOR SO–SO	Couldn't you walk the rope tight?
TOMMY HANDLEY	Not Blondin likely. Later on I became a sealion tamer.
Horace Percival	On dry land?
TOMMY HANDLEY	No — in a tank. I learned to catch a kipper in my kisser, as they were thrown at me. Sometimes people threw coins.
THE DIVER	Every penny makes the water warmer, sir.
TOMMY HANDLEY	How did that diver get in here?
THE DIVER	I'm going out now, sir.
F/X	**BUBBLES**
TOMMY HANDLEY	Shine the lamp, Sam. Leaving the circus I went on the stage as a contortionist.
Dorothy Summers	What's that?

TOMMY HANDLEY	A twister.
Fred Yule	Who is?
TOMMY HANDLEY	I is — was.
Fred Yule	You still are.
TOMMY HANDLEY	Wo-ho. One evening as I thrust my head through my legs to pick up a handkerchief which was sticking out of the conductor's tail-coat pocket I strained my imagination . . .
Clarence Wright	Ours is getting a bit bent.
TOMMY HANDLEY	So I was forced to retire from the Halls and resort to the theatre proper. From playing small parts I rapidly advanced and so at the early age of seventy-two I was playing leads.
Fred Yule	Didn't you ever play Preston?
TOMMY HANDLEY	No, the match was cancelled. Suddenly film offers were showered upon me.
Clarence Wright	Showered upon me.
OMNES	Showered upon me, showered upon me.
TOMMY HANDLEY	Quiet! I starred in many films. I played the divot in 'The Good Earth', but was replaced later. Then the empty clothes-line in 'Gone With The Wind', and finished up with a good fat part of the frying pan in 'Mr Chips'. And now, having reached the pinnacle of my profession, I look back on my career and I say to myself —
MRS MOPP	Ta-ta for now.
TOMMY HANDLEY	Perhaps you're right. Douse the lamp, Sam.
ORCHESTRA	**FANFARE UP AND UNDER**
Jack Train	Tom mumbles on!
ORCHESTRA	**FANFARE UP AND OUT**
TOMMY HANDLEY	I'd better get along and see how the funfair is progressing.
F/X	**DOOR OPENS**
COMMERCIAL TRAVELLER	Good morning.

TOMMY HANDLEY	Good morning.
TRAVELLER	*Grand* day.
TOMMY HANDLEY	Yes.
TRAVELLER	Any coconuts, teddy bears or hooplas?
TOMMY HANDLEY	No, thank you. Hey you, I thought you'd been called up?
TRAVELLER	Yes, but now I'm called back. Grand morning, *great* day.
F/X	**DOOR CLOSES**
TOMMY HANDLEY	That was Reg Ected. Band — Fanfare to the Funfair.
ORCHESTRA	**MUSIC LINK FADING INTO FAIRGROUND NOISES**
TOMMY HANDLEY	By Jove, Bookham's done a grand job. The moment I saw this fair I said to myself —
SAM SCRAM	Walk up! Walk up! The greatest show on earth!
TOMMY HANDLEY	Ah, there you are Bookham. Good work.
BOOKHAM	Glad you like it. Look at this — the laziest lion in captivity. Go into the cage, Mr Mayor — he won't touch you.
F/X	**GATE OPENS, LONG ROAR**
TOMMY HANDLEY	That sounds familiar.
MAN (Fred Yule)	I'll say it does, old boy, old boy — splendid grub, too.
TOMMY HANDLEY	Well, I'll chew a cheetah. It's Willy Nilly with a navy blue nose.
MAN	Too tired to talk — so long.
F/X	**GATE CLOSES**
TOMMY HANDLEY	Throw him a bone, Sam.
BOOKHAM	And here's another winner, Mr Mayor — a smasher. Handcuffio, the great escapologist. He can get out of anything.
TOMMY HANDLEY	A man after my own heart.
BOOKHAM	See — I tie him hand and foot with a hood over his head.

TOMMY HANDLEY	Well, manacle his ankles.
F/X	**HANDCUFFS**
TOMMY HANDLEY	That's right. Screw his legs together — tie his ears behind in a bow. Glue his arms down and nail him in that iron chest.
F/X	**HAMMERING, ETC.**
TOMMY HANDLEY	Hang a Christopher Stone round his neck and if he gets out of that in record time, my name's Roy Rich.
BOOKHAM	With one mighty bound he leaps from his living tomb.
F/X	**CLATTER**
SIGNOR SO–SO	Violà!
TOMMY HANDLEY	He's out! Why, it's Houdino Galvani. What are you doing in that chest, So-So?
SO–SO	Notting at all, notting at all.
TOMMY HANDLEY	Well, I'll ring up Whitehall 1212.
BOOKHAM	Now see our shooting gallery. The greatest sensation of all time. They don't use rifles — they use machine guns. Look, they're practising.
F/X	**MACHINE GUN**
LEFTY	Aim for the whites of the eggs, Sam.
SAM SCRAM	Aw, Lefty, I can't use one of dem things. Gimme a sawn off short gun.
LEFTY	Here come two bozos — try it on dem.
SAM	Don't shoot, Lefty. It's the Mayor and his agent.
LEFTY	What's Mayors to me? What's agents neither? I bin after dose guys for years.
SAM	Don't shoot, Lefty.
LEFTY	I got the gun — they're going to get the woiks.
F/X	**MACHINE GUN**
LEFTY	Missed 'em!
SAM	I thought you were a dead shot with one of dem tings.

LEFTY	Aw — it's me noives, I tell ya — it's me noives.
TOMMY HANDLEY	Hello, this is interesting. Fanny Fleshbaum, the fattest filly in Foaming-at-the-Mouth. I'll have a few stone of this. Gosh, she's enormous. I'll talk to her to see which of those chins is her mouth. Tell me, Fanny, have you a message for the Mayor?
MRS MOPP	Can I do you now, sir?
TOMMY HANDLEY	Mrs Mopp, who's been blowing you up? Here — Bookham's slipped me a fast one. All these freaks are my staff.
ALI OOP	You buy nice guide to funfair? Very saucy, very special.
TOMMY HANDLEY	Not you, hummer. Pipe down.
ALI OOP	I pipe down — I pipe back.
BOOKHAM	This way, Mr Mayor. The biggest money spinner you ever saw. A roundabout — real horses. The faster they go the better you like it. They fling you onto a chute and the chute shoots you into the lake. It's a sensation!
TOMMY HANDLEY	Sounds awful to me. Start her up, Sam.
ORCHESTRA	**ROUNDABOUT MUSIC, GAINING SPEED UNDER**

COMMERCIAL TRAVELLER	Good morning. *Nice* day.
MAN	Hello, old boy, old boy.
MRS MOPP	Can I do you now, sir?
TOMMY HANDLEY	Shine the lamp, sir.
LEFTY	He's a great guy, a great guy.
SIGNOR SO–SO	I kiss you hello.
Kay Cavendish & Paula Green	*(scream)*
THE DIVER	I'm going round now, sir.
SAM SCRAM	Boss, boss — sumpin' terrible's going to happen!
F/X	**BUMP AND SLIDE**
BOOKHAM	There you are. Down the chute — into the lake.
F/X	**SPLASH**
TOMMY HANDLEY	Every penny makes the water warmer!
ORCHESTRA	**SIGNATURE TUNE TO FINISH**

In March of 1942, while the Foaming-at-the-Mouth series was still running, Tommy Handley received a letter from the King's Equerry stating that the Royal Family would like ITMA to come to Windsor Castle to give a performance on Princess Elizabeth's sixteenth birthday. The invitation was a particular tribute to the entire hard-working team, for there had never before been a Royal Command Radio Show. The date was 21 April and, under the strictest secrecy, Francis Worsley and Ted Kavanagh began to make preparations. The show was to last for two hours; since the normally thirty-minute ITMA format could be stretched to forty at the most, a number of other variety artistes were asked to join the evening's programme—Robb Wilton, with his Home Guard sketch, Jack Warner, then at the Garrison Theatre, the Forces' sweetheart Vera Lynn, the double-act of Kenway and Young, and Max Geldray with his harmonica.

The theme of the ITMA contribution was that Tommy Handley was having a birthday party. A visit to Windsor by Ted Kavanagh beforehand and chats between Handley and the members of the Household between rehearsals and during lunch provided a sufficient number of nicknames, individual characteristics, and general domestic gossip to sprinkle through the already apposite script.

The performance (given precisely as it would be in a radio studio, at Their Majesties' request) was a huge success, and it was obvious that the members of the Royal Family were keen ITMA fans. This was confirmed after the show, when performers, producer, writer, and compere (John Snagge) were invited to meet their Royal audience. The Queen, hearing from Tommy Handley that there would be a new series after the summer break, rejoined with 'Ah, you go—you come back!', and Jack Train later told of the Gentleman of the Royal Household who remarked that if the war were to end between 8.30 and 9.00 on a Thursday night, none of the Household would dare to tell King George until ITMA had finished.

Once the excitement of the visit to Windsor Castle had receded, it was time to begin planning the next series. The setting was once again Foaming-at-the-Mouth, but the village had now been graced with a war factory, predictably managed by Handley. The presence of the factory, at a time when civilians across the country were channeling all their energies into the war effort, marked the beginning of a conscious policy to make ITMA topical, to relate the scripts to current conditions and feelings. It was never quite made clear what, if anything, this particular factory was producing—certainly none of its employees knew—but the jargon was real, culled from a trip through the Wellington Bomber Works at Chester by writer and producer.

The characters from the previous two series adapted themselves to a manufacturing life, and even Funf paid an occasional visit. When he did, he was accompanied by Johann Bull (Fred Yule), a hearty, cheerful spy who amused himself with explosives and insisted on having his 'little chokes'. Three other new voices were Yule's Norman the Doorman ('vicky-verky'), Bookham the Variety Agent (Jack Train) who inserted h's into most of his words, and the Man from the Ministry (Clarence Wright)—almost as vaguely defined in terms of what he did as the factory itself, and saddled with the habit of repeating the last word of every phrase he uttered. But the best-remembered addition to the ITMA community would be Jack Train's bibulous Colonel Chinstrap. A lovable mixture of roguishness and dignity, the Colonel would continue his dogged pursuit of liquid refreshment until the very last broadcast in 1949. And thirty years later his catchphrase 'I don't mind if I do' is still frequently heard in response to an invitation to drink.

The series ended on 29 January, but before that another landmark was passed in terms of wartime radio: on 6 November 1942 the programme was relayed by shortwave to the Forces in the Middle East and West Africa, a significant extension of ITMA's audience at a time when troops were massing for El Alamein.

Fred Yule

Alias
Johann Bull
Norman the Doorman
Andrew Geekie
George Gorge
Bigga Banga
Atlas

Remembers

It seems almost impossible to realise that a quarter of a century has passed since we all stood on the stage in the Paris Cinema and sang 'It's That Man Again', our signature tune. One line of this ran, 'Mother's pride and joy, Mrs Handley's boy,' and I feel sure that thousands of mothers in many parts of the world would have been proud of our Tommy as *their* boy.

No stage impressionist has ever truly captured the chuckling voice and the warm friendliness that emanated from him—I never knew him to lose his temper with anyone. We were a happy party and the spontaneous wit from Tommy and the laughter of a packed audience made us proud to be part of ITMA.

One of the longest laughs I can remember came when 'Frisby Dyke' (Deryck Guyler, who had grown a temporary beard) tried to answer a question from Tommy in a broad Liverpool dialect. Tommy paused for a second, then replied, 'Frisby! You stand there, looking like the brush hanging outside the little window.' He got no further! The audience got the allusion at once and it dried everyone up with laughter, Deryck included, for over a minute. Incidentally, it was not long before Deryck was clean shaven.

At every performance we had VIPs in the audience, but to Tommy *everyone* was equal. I can recall one occasion when, just before the show began and the audience was coming in, he was chatting to a member of the Royal Family. A little man entered, followed by his wife, and Tommy immediately said to H.R.H., 'Excuse me, Sir, I must show that lady and gentleman to their seats.' They were the paper sellers from the street corner, to whom he had given a couple of tickets for the show.

You may have heard this story before, but it shows the 'unflappability' of Tommy. We were doing a show in one of the cities up north and it necessitated staying overnight in a hotel. Tommy asked for an early call. In the morning there was a loud knock on his bedroom door and a tousle-headed youth popped his head inside and said, 'Are you the feller as wanted calling at 7.30?' 'Yes,' said Tommy. 'Well, it's quarter past eight.' One might have expected annoyance—but as usual Tommy saw the funny side, and burst out laughing.

Nowadays, when I feel down, I just look at the photograph of him, which has pride of place in our house, and I can always hear that friendly voice and his usual greeting, 'Hello Folks'.

Fred Yule

The Fougasse series of posters (*middle right*) was a constant reminder of the presence of informers, and encouraged the spirit and obstinacy (*right*) shown throughout the country.

Don't forget that walls have ears!

CARELESS TALK COSTS LIVES

Above, Horace Percival's Diver takes orders from the Mayor; *right*, the wartime ITMA cast: from left to right, Clarence Wright, Fred Yule, Dorothy Summers, Sydney Keith, Tommy Handley, Paula Green, Jack Train, Kay Cavendish, Dino Galvani.

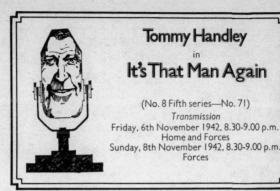

Tommy Handley

in

It's That Man Again

(No. 8 Fifth series—No. 71)
Transmission
Friday, 6th November 1942, 8.30-9.00 p.m.
Home and Forces
Sunday, 8th November 1942, 8.30-9.00 p.m.
Forces

ANNOUNCER	Well, ladies and gentlemen, for the first time tonight this ITMA programme is going out on the short wave to the Forces in the Middle East and West Africa. Glad to have you with us, boys, and now, everybody at home and abroad, pray silence for Tommy Handley — Yes, 'It's That Man Again!'
ORCHESTRA	**SIGNATURE TUNE**
OMNES	It's that man again, Yes, that man again, Yes sir, Tommy Handley is here —
ANNOUNCER	His factory is in the course of erection. He himself is in course of ejection but although something terrible is always happening he's still —
OMNES	Mother's pride and joy, Mrs Handley's boy, Oh it's useless to complain — When trouble's brewing, it's his doing, That man, that man again!
F/X	**GAVEL**
Fred Yule	Pray silence for your Chairman and Managing Director, the Right Rumbumptious Tommy Handley!
F/X	**INCREASED HAMMERING**
TOMMY HANDLEY	It's all right, boys — you can knock off now.
	(cheers and applause)

How on earth can they hear me out in the Middle East if you're making all that row? Well, folks, my factory is nearly finished. The roof is just being tiled and as my foreman remarked, 'That's put the lid on it'. I'm just going out on the tiles and —

F/X	**PHONE**
TOMMY HANDLEY	Hello?
HARI KARI (Jack Train)	*(jabber)*
TOMMY HANDLEY	Oh, you've decided to move have you? About time , too.
HARI KARI	*(jabber)*
TOMMY HANDLEY	Oh, you can't help yourself — fine.
HARI KARI	*(jabber)*
TOMMY HANDLEY	You can't stop? Well, I warned you.
HARI KARI	*(jabber)*
F/X	**CLICK**
TOMMY HANDLEY	Hullo? Blimey, he's been cut off. That was a running commentary by Rommel on a camel. Up to now the Department has been most helpful in assisting my building operations. Here's the latest form they've sent me to fill in. It's marked 'Strictly Confidential', so I'll read it out. It says: 'Further to our previous order Whitehall 1212 C.O.D. 1942 N.B.G. substitute Schedule R.O.T. para. 765. If the roof of your factory be higher than the floor, fill in column B.O.G.619 A to Z, but if the floor be higher than the roof substitute Government Order S.O.S. Q.E.D. 999. How are you?' That's easy — I could do it standing on my head. In fact, that's the only way I could do it.
F/X	**DOOR OPENS**
SAM SCRAM (Sydney Keith)	Boss, boss, sumpin' terrible's happened!
TOMMY HANDLEY	What — don't tell me they've put us back to 8.30 Sunday morning?
SAM	No, boss, that Government Inspector's coming down today.
TOMMY HANDLEY	Who? Mr Squirt — I said Squirt. I don't mind seeing him now the building's nearly finished.

SAM	Well, boss, there's a lot of things he'll want to see.
TOMMY HANDLEY	You're right, Sam. Go down to the village and get me a dozen metamorphoses.
SAM	Sure, boss, sure. *(going off)* A dozen metamurfys. Well, for evermore!
F/X	**DOOR CLOSES**
TOMMY HANDLEY	Well, I'd better have a look round the works. I can't tell you what we're going to make there — it's so secret they haven't even told me. I'll get my architect, Signor So-So, to explain the layout.
F/X	**BUZZER**
TOMMY HANDLEY	Send in So-So, will you? Well, whatever he's doing tell him to stop it and come here.
F/X	**DOOR OPENS**
COMMERCIAL TRAVELLER (Clarence Wright)	*(sadly)* Good morning.
TOMMY HANDLEY	Good morning.
TRAVELLER	Nice day.
TOMMY HANDLEY	Yes.
TRAVELLER	Any false rumours, horrors or hangovers?
TOMMY HANDLEY	No, thank you.
TRAVELLER	I'll call again.
TOMMY HANDLEY	Do.
TRAVELLER	Good morning.
TOMMY HANDLEY	Good morning.
TRAVELLER	Shocking day.
F/X	**DOOR CLOSES**
TOMMY HANDLEY	That was Lou Gubrious. He's got a great sense of humour. Well, what's next?
F/X	**TELEPHONE**

TOMMY HANDLEY	Hello?
FUNF (Jack Train)	This is Funf speaking. Your factory will never open.
TOMMY HANDLEY	Who'll stop it?
FUNF	I will, my agents are everywhere.
TOMMY HANDLEY	They never get *me* any dates. I've been out since tea-time.
FUNF	I hate you, Handley, I hate you. Funf has spoken!
F/X	**RECEIVER IS REPLACED**
TOMMY HANDLEY	We'll have to call this show 'Friday Night at Hate'.
F/X	**KNOCK AT DOOR**
TOMMY HANDLEY	This'll be So-So. Come in.
F/X	**DOOR OPENS**
MRS MOPP (Dorothy Summers)	Can I do you now, sir?

TOMMY HANDLEY	Well, if it isn't Mrs Mopp the vamping vassal with the tousled tassel. I thought you told me you were called up?
MRS MOPP	Well, sir, I had me medical.
TOMMY HANDLEY	And were you passed A.1?
MRS MOPP	Oh no, sir. I'm passed sixty-two.
TOMMY HANDLEY	You don't look a day over sixty-one. I mean, were you passed fit?

MRS MOPP	Oh, I'm never passed it, sir.
TOMMY HANDLEY	I said, passed fit.
MRS MOPP	No, sir — I was examined by a lady doctor. She wanted me to remove my bonnet.
TOMMY HANDLEY	Disgraceful! I expect she wanted to open a false front.
MRS MOPP	I wouldn't let her meddle with my modesty vest, sir. I said, 'You must take me as you find me.' The Labour sent me to you, sir.
TOMMY HANDLEY	The Labour? That's capital. I'll put you in charge of the sock exchange.
MRS MOPP	Oh, thank you, sir. I brought this for you.
TOMMY HANDLEY	Isn't that nice. What is it — an engineer's indiscretion?
MRS MOPP	No, sir, it's an overseer's 'otpot.
TOMMY HANDLEY	Thank you, Mrs M. There'll be an 'otpot in the Old Tom tonight.
MRS MOPP	Ta-ta for now.
TOMMY HANDLEY	Tattoo me brow.
F/X	**DOOR CLOSES**
TOMMY HANDLEY	I'm sorry she's not going into the Army, we can do with plenty of tanks.
F/X	**DOOR OPENS**
Horace Percival	*(singing)* Down in the forest something stirred, It was only the note of a bird.
F/X	**DOOR CLOSES. BIRD SOUNDS**
TOMMY HANDLEY	Hey, you've forgotten the bird. I hope my new office in the factory will be proofed against all these interruptions. I can't write letters with pigeons pattering all over my pad and puffing my pipe and besides —
F/X	**DOOR OPENS. FIRE ENGINE UP**
CECIL (Horace Percival)	After you, Claude.
CLAUDE (Jack Train)	No — after *you*, Cecil.

TOMMY HANDLEY	What are you bringing that fire engine in here for?
CECIL	The curfew tolls, so you must leave this place —
CLAUDE	And we're afraid that you will have to flee.
CECIL	The situation you will have to face —
TOMMY HANDLEY	And leave the world to darkness and to me.
CLAUDE	Save that in yonder cupboard made of wood —
CECIL	A barrel lies concealed beneath the shelves.
CLAUDE	Shall we remove it while the going's good?
TOMMY HANDLEY	By all means, boys. Get busy, help yourselves.
CECIL	After you, Claude.
CLAUDE	No — after *you*, Cecil.
F/X	**ENGINE MOVES OUT. DOOR CLOSES**
TOMMY HANDLEY	That's put *them* out. And now to work.
F/X	**DOOR OPENS**
SIGNOR SO—SO (Dino Galvani)	Ah, Mr Candlepower, I am late but as the old adverb says, a stitch in time saves eight.
TOMMY HANDLEY	You mean, a soft palate turneth away broth. Now, what are you going to show me first?
SO—SO	First we will listen to the Works' Band playing on the stooge.
TOMMY HANDLEY	Playing on the stooge? He must be a strong man. You mean stage.
SO—SO	Yes, that is what I said. In the canteen they are going to play 'The Golloping Major'.
TOMMY HANDLEY	I suppose you'll accompany him on the glutton spiel.
SO—SO	But it has been arranged by Gordon Ja*cob*.
TOMMY HANDLEY	Gordon J. Cobb, the American? I know his pop Corn.
SO—SO	No, Gordon *Ja*cob.

TOMMY HANDLEY	Oh, that's different. But what's all this got to do with showing me round the factory?
SO–SO	Notting at all, notting at all.
TOMMY HANDLEY	Well, I'm not going to miss this for anything. Let the works wait.
SAM SCRAM	Boss! Here's a note from Charlie Shadwell.
TOMMY HANDLEY	What does he say? 'Feeling much baton. Dr Jacob came yesterday — took my tempo and clarinet my grapes.' He sounds as if he's getting better. Now who's going to follow the band today?
Frank Cantell	I am, Tommy.
TOMMY HANDLEY	Right. In the regretted absence of Charles Shadwell, the Works' Band under Foreman Frank will entertain you. Carry on Cantell.
ORCHESTRA	'THE GALLOPING MAJOR'
	(applause)
LEFTY (Jack Train)	Say, Sam, what's the big idea? Why can't the boss show *us* the works?
SAM	They're a secret, Lefty.
LEFTY	Aw — he gives me the willies. Dere ain't a decent racket left in dis dump.
JOHANN BULL (Fred Yule)	*(coming in)* Ach, guten morgen, gentlemen. For long have I wished to meet you?
SAM	Ah, howdy, Mr B — er —
JOHANN BULL	Bull — Johann Bull, that is my nome de spy.
LEFTY	Howya? You're a great spy — a great spy. What's cookin'?
JOHANN BULL	What is cooking? Ho ho — a nice hod-pod for you, Tommy. Ho ho. Yes — very hod-pod.
SAM	Gee, you ain't going to frame the boss, are you?
JOHANN BULL	Oh no — just a warm welcome for him in his factory. I would not hurt a flea. Come, have a spod with me, gentlemen.
SAM	Not me — I'm sticking to the boss. Don't go, Lefty. This guy's a phoney.
JOHANN BULL	Oh yes, I am very funny — I tell ya some good chokes.

LEFTY	I'd like to hear 'em. C'mon.
SAM	I'm not doin' anything doity, mind you.
LEFTY	It's his noives, you see. It's his noives.
JOHANN BULL	*(going off)* I will make it worth your vile. Ho ho ....
TOMMY HANDLEY	Who's that leaving my office? Looks like two men and a stoat. Now, So-So, you are an architect, aren't you?
SO–SO	Oh yes, Mr Hagglemuch. I am an unqualified artichoke. I have built many sky scrappers, and bolks of falts.
TOMMY HANDLEY	Bolks of falts?
SO–SO	Yes – luxury falts.
TOMMY HANDLEY	Now listen, you leaning tower of Pisa, you can say bolks of falts as easy as I can.
SO–SO	You mean blocks of flats. I have also built a villain in the country.
TOMMY HANDLEY	A villain?
SO–SO	Yes, a semi-detached villain.
TOMMY HANDLEY	Sounds like an actor with a bad memory.
F/X	**DOOR OPENS**
SO–SO	Come this way. This is your office. I will finish it.
TOMMY HANDLEY	Listen, So-So, leave the finishing – er – furnishing of this to me. Any more of your basic English and I'd go mad.
SO–SO	Oka-da-doke.

TOMMY HANDLEY	Ice-a da cream.
F/X	**DOOR CLOSES**
TOMMY HANDLEY	So this is my new office, eh? It's a big improvement on my old Mayor's parlour. I'll throw a few parties in here. I'll throw a few out as well —
F/X	**DOOR OPENS**
CECIL	Is this the new Manager's office?
TOMMY HANDLEY	Don't ask me, I'm only a novice.
CECIL	We've come to lay lino.
CLAUDE	That's right, me old chino.
CECIL	Our boss a bit of a teff is —
CLAUDE	And we've got an order official.
CECIL	To ignore it means instant dismissal.
TOMMY HANDLEY	I've heard nothing dafter, It's a bonus you're after —
CECIL	You, Claude.
CLAUDE	No — after *you*, Cecil.
F/X	**DOOR CLOSES**
TOMMY HANDLEY	A policeman at Lewisham Junction Who once used his truncheon with unction, When he — Oh, they've gone. I wonder what's through that door?
F/X	**DOOR OPENS**
TOMMY HANDLEY	Oh, a private bathroom — and a shower. I like that. I'll pull the string and see if it works. I hope it won't let the pigeons out.
F/X	**RUNNING WATER**
TOMMY HANDLEY	That's fine, I'll have a bath now. I'll take my coat off and get in — I've got waterproof trousers on.
F/X	**DOOR CLOSES. SPLASHING NOISES**

(Tommy starts to sing 'Boom, boom, boom' etc., is joined by quartet singing 'Oh, where is the loofah?', then singing fades.)

JOHANN BULL   Ach, mein lieber Lefty, in the bath is Herr Handley so on his office table I w put the time bomb. It will blow him high sky.

LEFTY   De big bozo'll tink someone's given him a clock.

F/X   **TICKING**

JOHANN BULL   Ja, ja. He will be off in a tick, hein? Ho, ho — I must have my little choke. L us get out before it goes off.

F/X   **MORE SPLASHES. DOOR OPENS**

TOMMY HANDLEY   Hi, you two, what's all this?

JOHANN BULL   Guten tag, mein friendt. A small present have I brought you. Goodbye.

F/X   **TICKING GETS FASTER**

TOMMY HANDLEY   No, don't go, I've got a funny story I want to tell you.

JOHANN BULL   Some other time.

TOMMY HANDLEY   It's a lovely story about two men and a bomb.

JOHANN BULL   Nein, I must go.

F/X   **TELEPHONE**

TOMMY HANDLEY   Excuse me. I've got to go to answer the phone.

F/X   **DOOR IS CLOSED AND LOCKED. CRIES OF 'LET ME OUT, LET ME OL THEN EXPLOSION**

JOHANN BULL   *(going up)* It was just a little choke.

LEFTY   *(in distance)* It's a great sky — a great sky.

TOMMY HANDLEY   Drop in some time and I'll finish the story.

F/X   **DOOR OPENS**

SAM SCRAM   Boss, boss, dat guy's plotting sumpin' against you.

TOMMY HANDLEY   I know he's up to something.

SAM	And sumpin' else, boss — they're sending a guy from the BBC to broadcast your factory at work.
TOMMY HANDLEY	We'd better prepare for him, Sam. Get me some Salama vac-chat and a couple of decibels, will you?
SAM	Sure, boss, sure. *(going off)* What did he say? A couple of Jessabels and a silly almanack — for evermore!
F/X	**DOOR OPENS**
Kay Cavendish	Oh, hello, Tommy, is this your new office?
TOMMY HANDLEY	Hello, girls. How do you like it?
Paula Green	There isn't room to swing a cat in it.
TOMMY HANDLEY	Well, that doesn't matter. I haven't got a cat to swing. And talking of swing, what about some hot doggerel.
KAY CAVENDISH, PAULA GREEN, & ORCHESTRA	**'DADDY WOULDN'T BUY ME A BOW-WOW'**
	(applause)
SAM SCRAM	Boss, boss, as I was on my way to get your silly almanack I met the Inspector. He's coming to the factory right away.
TOMMY HANDLEY	I'll have to give him a drink, Sam, so get a bottle of cucharacha — the cooking cucharacha, remember — and a syphon of sphagnum.
SAM	A syphon of sphagnum?
TOMMY HANDLEY	Yes. Don't I make it clear? A syphon of sphagnum and a sizzle stick.
SAM	What do you want a sizzle stick for?
TOMMY HANDLEY	For evermore!
F/X	**DOOR CLOSES**
TOMMY HANDLEY	I'll fool the Inspector this time. I'll take him round so fast that he'll see the same thing seven times.
F/X	**DOOR OPENS**
BOOKHAM (Jack Train)	Good news for you, Mr H. Great good news.

TOMMY HANDLEY	What, have you heard from the Middle East already?
BOOKHAM	Better still, Mr H. Your film is a smasher — it's a tear-up.
BOTH	It's a wo-how?
BOOKHAM	I've organised a grand ga-hala performance.
TOMMY HANDLEY	Every seat is boo-hooked?
BOOKHAM	Sta-halls, ci-hircle and ga-hallery.
TOMMY HANDLEY	Sple-hendid. Put on a couple of news reels, 'Gone with the Wind', and a tall hat and I'll meet you down there.
BOOKHAM	You'll be de-ligh-hited, Mr H. *(going away)* It's a smasher!
F/X	**DOOR CLOSES**
TOMMY HANDLEY	I'll bet it's a dud. He'll probably put on 'The Birth of a Nation' with new dialogue.
F/X	**DOOR OPENS**
INSPECTOR SQUIRT (Clarence Wright)	Now look here, Handley — I said Handley.
TOMMY HANDLEY	Tomitma to you, Mr Squirt — I said Itma.
INSPECTOR	My Department insists that you start production right away — I said away.
TOMMY HANDLEY	I'll surprise you, Mr Squirt — I said surprise you. The whole factory is in working order.
INSPECTOR	You do surprise me — I said surprise me. When I left home this morning I said to the wife —
TOMMY HANDLEY	I'll be late tonight, dear, my secretary's a very nice girl. Now, before you tour the works I want you to see my new film.
INSPECTOR	I've no time for films, sir.
TOMMY HANDLEY	You'll have time for this one. Grab him, boys.
CECIL	After you, Cecil — I said Claude.
CLAUDE	No — after *you*, Claude — I said Cecil.

TOMMY HANDLEY	To the Handleydrome, led by Muriel Dry —
ORCHESTRA	COMEDY SEQUENCE
NORMAN (Fred Yule)	High time you was here, sir. They're fair frantic — or vicky verky.
TOMMY HANDLEY	That's nothing to what they'll be later, Norman. Be ready to catch me as I come out — or vicky verky.
ORCHESTRA	FANFARE
Fred Yule	*(invigorated)* Foaming British Films —
ORCHESTRA	CHORD
Clarence Wright	Present the ITMA Factory Film Unit Production
ORCHESTRA	CHORD
Sydney Keith	'From Nuts to Bolts!'
ORCHESTRA	CHORD
Jack Train	It's a Handley H'Epic!
ORCHESTRA	FANFARE
TOMMY HANDLEY	Today without fear or flavour I present a day in the life of my mass-production factory, where we make everything from Wardens' Posts to whoopee. Here is a typical shift arriving punctually from eight to ten a.m. or thereabouts. As they clock in, see how happy they are.
F/X	CLOCKING IN
Horace Percival	Here — I'll clock you if you punch my card.
Jack Train	Nark it or I'll punch you right in the clock.
	(general uproar)
Fred Yule	Who do you think you are, Lord Nuffield? Go on, get out of it —
TOMMY HANDLEY	Laughing and joking, happy as sandboys they enter the factory. In they march to the stirring strains of a popular tune — the song of the moment.
ORCHESTRA	'LAZYBONES' UP AND OUT

TOMMY HANDLEY	Before joining them in the nap I want to tell you I make a point of knowing each of my workers personally, and so I have a cheery word for each of them. Listen — Morning, Phyllis?
Paula Green	That's enough of that. For two pins I'd leave the blinking place.
TOMMY HANDLEY	Charming girl. I must put another penny in her pay packet. Now I greet another worker. And how's tricks, Charlie?
Fred Yule	Oh, go and chase yourself round the boiler house.
TOMMY HANDLEY	You see, they all love and respect me. I'm not only their guv'nor, I'm their best friend. They come to me with all their troubles.
Horace Percival	Hey, Handley — what about paying me my last week's wages?
TOMMY HANDLEY	Not too loud, George — they'll all want their money.
Horace Percival	Well, what about it?
TOMMY HANDLEY	Give me a chance George. I must wait and see if my football coupons come up.
Horace Percival	Blimey. What'll I say to the missus?
TOMMY HANDLEY	Tell her I picked your pocket while you were working.
F/X	**KLAXON**
TOMMY HANDLEY	Morning tea is now served, usually with a little entertainment by our Works' Band, The Swing Hammers. I'm very proud of this band — no other factory has anything like it, except the Silver Wedding Band from Much Wedlock. Here they are in a typical selection.
ORCHESTRA	**SWING NUMBER**
TOMMY HANDLEY	As I was saying, no wonder no other factory has anything like it. The staff usually dance to this band until lunchtime. I usually take a turn with one of them myself. Excuse me, miss, will you take a turn for the worse?
ORCHESTRA	**'BLUE DANUBE' WITH EFFECTS**
TOMMY HANDLEY	What is that noise? You sound as if you were enjoying yourself.
MRS MOPP	I am sir. Me corsets is fair creakin'.
TOMMY HANDLEY	You'd better go out and get oiled.

ORCHESTRA	**ENDING SEQUENCE**
TOMMY HANDLEY	Now I usually allow two hours for lunch during which I stage a floorshow featuring a well-known act, such as those famous cross-talk comedians, To and From. Here they are in a characteristic excerpt from their repertoire.
TRUMPET & TROMBONE	**COMIC CROSS-TALK**
VOICE	*(trombone under)* Who was the lady I saw you with last night?
VOICE	*(trumpet under)* That wasn't a lady. That was my wife.
TOMMY HANDLEY	It sounds worse as a trio. This year my work-people are putting on an oriental musical com. ¹v — 'The Workhaido'. Here is the opening chorus. Words by the foreman. Music by the Five Women.
OMNES	We're so happy to be working in the Itma factor-ee, You won't find us idly lurking In a place we shouldn't be, Give three cheers for Handley, hurray, hurrah, hurray — He treats us so grandly, hurrah, hurray, hurrah, And while he does us all inspire We won't set the works on fire — hurrire, hurrire, hurrire.
TOMMY HANDLEY	Charming lyric, isn't it? Copies of this song may be had in lieu of wages. Now, as the sun sinks over the chimney, I say farewell to my weary toilers in the factory where our motto is 'We All Work Like Fun, But We Like Fun Best'.
ORCHESTRA	**LONG FANFARE**
Jack Train	'Tom Turns it Off!'
SAM SCRAM	Boss, the BBC bloke has arrived. He wants you to take him round the works to rehearse the broadcast.
TOMMY HANDLEY	All right — as long as it doesn't interfere with production. What are we making at present?
SAM	I don't know, boss.
TOMMY HANDLEY	I'll have to think something up. Where is he?
SAM	In the canteen, boss.
TOMMY HANDLEY	All right — wheel him in. And Sam?

SAM	Yeah, boss?
TOMMY HANDLEY	Keep that Inspector out of the way and chain up the moose.
SAM	Sure, boss, sure.
F/X	**DOOR CLOSES**
TOMMY HANDLEY	Now, if I can get this BBC commentator on the run he'll leave Michael standing.
F/X	**DOOR OPENS**
SAM	Here y'are, boss. Here he is.
PRATTLE (Jack Train)	Er — morning, Handley.
TOMMY HANDLEY	Good morning Mr — er — Mr — er —
PRATTLE	Prattle's the name. Outside Broadcasting. O.B., as we call it.
TOMMY HANDLEY	Oh, you're an O.B., are you? I often wondered what one looked like.
PRATTLE	I've heard some of your broadcasts, Handley. Quite good — some of them.
TOMMY HANDLEY	Or vicky verky. Now what's the game — I mean what would you like to do, Mr Prattle?
PRATTLE	We're anxious to broadcast your works in full swing.
TOMMY HANDLEY	Get the cards out — I mean I'll get my band out.
PRATTLE	I just want to get the lie of the land, so to speak.
TOMMY HANDLEY	Oh, I'll give you the lie all right. Come this way, Mr Brittle — er — Tattle.
PRATTLE	By the way, what are you making here?
TOMMY HANDLEY	It's a secret, Mr Prattle, but I can tell you *(whispers)*.
PRATTLE	Oh, really — you don't mean to tell me you've made —
TOMMY HANDLEY	Ssh! Careless prattle, Mr Talk.
PRATTLE	Quite, quite. Now, I'd like to meet some of your workers.
TOMMY HANDLEY	Set the alarm, Sam. Here is Mr Faceache, our foreman — a very ready talker.

PRATTLE	So you're the foreman?
FOREMAN (Fred Yule)	I ahm.
PRATTLE	Are you willing to give me a résumé of your work?
FOREMAN	Ahm nort.
TOMMY HANDLEY	You're keen on intensive production, aren't you? *(sotto)* Say yes.
FOREMAN	I ahm.
PRATTLE	Of course you're willing to tell listeners all about it.
TOMMY HANDLEY	Say no.
FOREMAN	Ahm nort.
PRATTLE	We're not getting very far. Are you nervous in front of the microphone?
TOMMY HANDLEY	Say no.
FOREMAN	I ahm.
TOMMY HANDLEY	And you're happy in your work? Say yes.
FOREMAN	Ahm nort.
TOMMY HANDLEY	That's funny, he knew his lines in the digs this morning. *(quickly)* Here you see, Mr Prattle, our main assembly shop.
F/X	**ROAR OF MACHINERY TO DROWN SPEECH**
TOMMY HANDLEY	*(on fade)* And it all depends on the fulcrum.
PRATTLE	Quite, quite.
	(chatter and laughs)
TOMMY HANDLEY	Quiet everyone, quiet. You see the molten metal is delivered to the suscansion through this panjoint pipe.
F/X	**BUBBLES**
THE DIVER (Horace Percival)	Don't forget the diver, sir.

PRATTLE	What was that?
TOMMY HANDLEY	He said it solididifies in the sempervivor borgyvor — that's part of pettyfog.
PRATTLE	Quite, quite.
OMNES	Quite, quite.
TOMMY HANDLEY	Quiet all of you, quiet.
PRATTLE	I'd like a word with that lady over there. What is her capacity?
TOMMY HANDLEY	About seven quarts. Miss Quail, this O.B. gent wants to speak to you.
MRS MOPP	I never speak to strange gentlemen — you should know that, Mr Tom.
TOMMY HANDLEY	But he wants you to broadcast.
MRS MOPP	Oh no, I've been caught like that before. One night in the blackout a gentleman came up to me, very well-spoken he was too, and he said 'Hello ducks, would you like to go on the air and —
PRATTLE	Quite, quite. Now a word with that blacksmith fellow. Can you describe in your own words your daily task?
ALI OOP	Please mister. I sell you blueprint very secret — very saucy, very, very blue.
TOMMY HANDLEY	*(loudly)* And here we have our conveyor system —
F/X	**CONVEYOR BELT STARTING UP**
PRATTLE	Oh, I see. An endless belt.
TOMMY HANDLEY	Quite, quite. *(sotto)* Loose the moose, Sam —
PRATTLE	Er — what is this curious article being delivered on the conveyor?
TOMMY HANDLEY	Eh? I'm afraid I can't see from where I'm standing.
COMMERCIAL TRAVELLER	*(coming in)* Good morning. *Nice* day *(laughs)*.
F/X	**BELLOW**
TOMMY HANDLEY	Take cover, Prattle old man, our mascot's making his morning call.
F/X	**BELLOW**

PRATTLE	But where can I go?
TOMMY HANDLEY	Hop on the endless belt with the others. Come on . . .
F/X	**BELLOW**
	(fade on general confusion)
ANNOUNCER	I must apologise that there is a temporary breakdown in the ITMA service. Until we can resume next week, here is a record —
ORCHESTRA	**SIGNATURE TUNE TO FINISH**

Good morning . . .
Nice day . . .

By the summer of 1943 the North African campaign had reached an end. July saw the fall of Mussolini, and in August the Russians began to push back the German eastern front. Reports from abroad indicated an eventual allied victory, news that replaced the nation's fears with a widespread feeling of impatience. But the new mood was a mixed one—the people's optimism was pervaded by a certain gloom that a triumph for national identity would provide a future which was not much better than the past.

During this time, ITMA was broadcasting its last summer season: from autumn '43 until the series ended early in '49 the programmes were on a fixed autumn to spring run of thirty-five or forty shows. The factory at Foaming-at-the-Mouth was transformed into a spa, a hotel, a holiday camp, all of them cheerful settings which coincided with the good war news. Clarence Wright had left to go on a roadshow, and Bill Stephens joined the cast as Comical Chris, a perpetual joker. Horace Percival added Mr Whats 'isname to his repertoire, an annoyingly inarticulate character based on someone Handley had met in London. Musical numbers in the programmes were by now all specially arranged and in addition to providing the traditional break they often had new lyrics by Kavanagh which were relevant to the storyline. The series ended on 5 August with the one hundredth ITMA broadcast.

After a short break another series began in September. Since the worst of the raids were thought to be over, the Variety Department had moved back to London and the new ITMA programmes were broadcast from the Criterion Theatre. Jack Train was ill during this series—which meant the temporary absence of Colonel Chinstrap—and, as a result of the first auditions ever to be given for ITMA, Jean Capra joined to become Poppy Poopah. By Christmas the format was firmly established and Handley presided as the Squire of Much-Fiddling Manor. Ironically, there was renewed bombing only five months after the move back to the Criterion. London sustained thirteen major raids between January and March 1944, all from larger and more destructive bombs than before, and centres like Hull and Bristol were the victims of a 'little blitz'.

It was during this series that ITMA gave special broadcasts for the Forces at home. At the invitation of the Admiralty, the entire team travelled to the Home Fleet base at Scapa Flow in January. During the five days they spent there they gave fifteen performances on ships and at shore stations, as well as recording a regular broadcast— aptly entitled 'H.M.S. Itma'. The success of the naval transmission led to an RAF edition in February, broadcast from the Criterion with an RAF audience, and, in April, a trip to the Garrison Theatre for an Army-orientated programme.

When the next series began in September of that year the war news was even better. Although German V2s were falling on London (and being explained away as 'gas mains exploding'), the allied invasion was progressing well and Montgomery had led the Second Army as far as Antwerp—overrunning the launching site for the V1 doodlebugs which had plagued London all summer. War industry was slacking off, black-out restrictions were soon to be relaxed, and civil defence units outside London were fast disappearing. Because the news was better, there were fewer war references in the broadcasts.

Jack Train's return brought back Colonel Chinstrap and introduced Mark Time, an ancient and depraved character who answered any query with 'I'll have to ask me Dad'. Diana Morrison, who had joined towards the end of the previous series, created Miss Hotchkiss, Handley's domineering secretary who was named after a machine gun. The series portrayed Tommy Handley with a 'plan' although, in the ITMA style, no one ever worked out quite what it was. Francis Worsley was in hospital for several months from Christmas and during this time script conferences were held at his bedside, while the studio production was carried out by Ronnie Waldman. But he was well and back at work in time to produce the triumphant Victory edition on 10 May. Europe was liberated, spirits were high, and ITMA celebrated with the rest of the country. The cavalcade returned to Foaming-at-the-Mouth for a victory parade, and paid a cheery tribute to 'the man with the big cigar'.

Molly Weir

Alias
Tattie Mackintosh
Mrs Mackintosh

Remembers

Although tickets were given out for ITMA, they didn't allocate actual seats, and those lucky enough to be given admission tickets used to queue for well over an hour before the doors opened, to be sure of getting as near to the stage as possible. This gave them an advantageous position for rushing us at the end for autographs, and also let them see every smile, grimace or frown at the closest possible range. One night, when Tommy had a bad dose of laryngitis, which had grown worse as the afternoon rehearsal proceeded, Francis Worsley decided at almost the eleventh hour to cancel the performance.

Anyway, when I got outside the fog was thickening, and on my way to the bus I met a great many people clutching the familiar ITMA cards. Thinking to save them a fruitless visit to the Paris only to be told there was no show, I breezed up to each one and said, 'ITMA has been cancelled —there's no show tonight, Tommy has a sore throat.' They stared at me disbelievingly. It had never missed a performance in the entire war. I was obviously a nut case who wanted their tickets! Clutching the precious slips of cardboard more firmly than ever, they hurried away from me, and not even my obviously Scottish voice convinced them they were speaking to Tattie. I couldn't help laughing that my friendly concern had been so misunderstood, and only hoped they'd get tickets for another night to make up for their disappointment. But I doubted it, for they were in great demand and allocated weeks in advance.

Another example of how people don't listen to the evidence of their own ears came one night when, after the show, a man came down for an autograph and said the part he had specially enjoyed that evening had been my performance as Naieve! Not only had I not played Naieve that night, but neither had anyone else, for that character had been dropped in the re-shuffle which had taken place at the end of the previous series!

Similarly, I was always being told how much people had enjoyed me saying 'Can I do you now, sir?' although that character also had been dropped before I joined and was played by Dolly Summers. Indeed, even someone at the BBC refused to believe I wasn't Mrs Mopp as recently as the fiftieth anniversary celebrations, when I was asked to appear in a show and discuss how I had played the part. Only when I told them to check with Equity that poor Dolly Summers was indeed dead and buried would they believe me. I think they thought I was being coy about having been in ITMA at all, all those years ago!

As if I would be so daft! I loved working with Tommy and aided and abetted him in all his teasing of my Scottish ways. Passing a cement mixer he would say, 'Do you know what that is, Tattie?' 'No, Tommy,' I'd answer. 'If it's not for mixing cement, I don't know what it is.' 'Mixing cement!' (this in tones of amazement). 'It's a haggis machine.' He told me long involved stories of a family of acrobats who travelled in an elastic-sided bus which stretched to accommodate their musical instruments, and this became almost a long-running serial on the bus journey we took to reach charity locations where we did performances. I was Tommy's 'straight man', and fed him all the expected questions, to the amusement of the rest of the company.

He loved any sort of dialect, and found the Scottish one very amusing. When it was decided to add another Scots voice to the show, I was not only Tattie, but became Tattie's mother as well. This involved me in long telephone conversations with myself, with Tommy butting in, and it became increasingly difficult to maintain my stiff-necked outraged cries of 'Och, it's awful, och, it's terrible', with Tommy darting back and forth and round me at the microphone. In the end I had to put up my script so that I couldn't see his face, or I'd have 'lost' the character completely.

I feel very fortunate that I had the great luck to become known to the English public through my work with one of the cleverest, kindest and most inspired comedians I have ever known. If I never did anything else on radio, to have been able to say 'I was in ITMA' would have been enough.

Molly Weir

Left, the cast embarks for its Army broadcast at the Garrison Theatre in a furniture van, the only transport available; *below*, from left to right, Dorothy Summers, Bryan Herbert, Tommy Handley, Paula Green, and Ted Kavanagh at a preliminary rehearsal.

Below left, Sam Scram gives Handley a polish before the Army transmission; *below right*, Handley and Mrs Mopp with flags out for V-E Day.

Tommy Handley

in

It's That Man Again

(No. 34 Eighth series—No. 172)
Transmission
Thursday, 10th May 1945, 8.30-9.00 p.m.
Home Service

ANNOUNCER	This is the BBC Home Service — VITMA!
ORCHESTRA	**FANFARE**
Fred Yule	Come on Foaming-at-Mouth, wave your flags —
Jean Capra	Somebody's just pinched mine.
ANNOUNCER	Yes — 'It's That Man Again!'
ORCHESTRA	**SIGNATURE TUNE**
OMNES	It's that man again, Yes, that man again, Yes sir, Tommy Handley is here!
Jack Train	*(American)* Calling all cars, calling all cars — keep a sharp lookout for suspicious character last seen heading north.
Fred Yule	Who is he?
OMNES	Mother's pride and joy Mrs Handley's boy, Oh, it's useless to complain — When trouble's brewing, it's his doing, That man, that man again.
1ST BOY (Jean Capra)	Get your catapults ready kids — he's going to speak from the balcony of the Town Hall.

2ND BOY (Clarence Wright)	I say — it's not very sporting of you chaps, is it?
1ST BOY	Cheese it Scruffy. Go and tell your mother she hates you.
2ND BOY	I think Handley's a jolly decent chap. He's going to give us a wizard time.
ORCHESTRA	**FANFARE**
1ST BOY	Look out! Here he is —
F/X	**WINDOW OPENS**
SAM SCRAM (Sydney Keith)	Ladies and gentlemen, I'm sorry to —
OMNES	We want Handley!
SAM	Owing to unforgivable circumstances, he ain't going to talk till tomorrow — *(general uproar)*
SAM	*(shouting over it)* It ain't my fault, is it? Come back tomorrow.
F/X	**WINDOW CLOSES**
SAM	Aw gee, I wish the boss'd keep his dates.
F/X	**DOOR OPENS**
TOMMY HANDLEY	Hello Sam — *(applause)*
TOMMY HANDLEY	Did you hear my speech Sam?
SAM	But boss, you never made it —
TOMMY HANDLEY	I did. I've been talking out of that window there.
SAM	But that one overlooks a field of cows.
TOMMY HANDLEY	Oh, I thought they looked like a matinée audience. Well, cows indeed — no wonder it was a flop.
SAM	Hey boss, you'll have to make another speech to the people.
TOMMY HANDLEY	No fear — I'm waiting till the town surrenders.

SAM	But boss, I saw the people crowning you with flowers.
TOMMY HANDLEY	Yes, but one fellow threw a shoe at me —
SAM	That was lucky boss.
TOMMY HANDLEY	Not for me. His old woman was still in it.
SAM	Look boss. There's someone coming in under a white flag. Shall I show him in?
TOMMY HANDLEY	No, I'll do a Monty on him — let 'im wait. Besides, I've got to prepare the instrument of surrender.
SAM	What's that boss?
TOMMY HANDLEY	That's a stocking full of railway station rock cakes.
SAM	Boss, you're not goin' to hit him as he comes in —
TOMMY HANDLEY	No, as he goes out. My motto is Nil Florence Desmond.
F/X	**DOOR OPENS**
THE MER (Jack Train)	This isn't fer, it isn't fer.
TOMMY HANDLEY	Who are you?
THE MER	The Mer.

TOMMY HANDLEY	The Mer? I don't ker if you are the Mer — take a cher, Mer.
THE MER	Wher?
TOMMY HANDLEY	Ther. Now, what's the trouble?
THE MER	All this worry, I cannot ber —
TOMMY HANDLEY	Ooh, you're suffering from wer and ter. Did such things happen when *I* was Mer?
SAM	Yeah —
TOMMY HANDLEY	Quiet cur. Now, Mr Mer, sign this and pull that chain off your neck.
THE MER	I protest, I decler.
TOMMY HANDLEY	But it's après la guer —
THE MER	Oh, but sper my grey hers.
TOMMY HANDLEY	Oh get up them sters —
F/X	**DOOR CLOSES**
TOMMY HANDLEY	Well now, Sam, I'll make my speech. Now sound a fanfer.
TRUMPET	**COMIC FLOURISH**
TOMMY HANDLEY	That's all fan and no fur. Give me that trumpet and I'll show you how to blow it.
F/X	**SIREN SOUND**
SAM	Take cover, boss —
TOMMY HANDLEY	Oh don't worry, Sam. It's Hess going home.
SAM	What about the speech boss?
TOMMY HANDLEY	Oh, the speech. Well, get me a cigar and a new set of Victory fingers and I'll speak at three o'clock.
SAM	Three o'clock boss?
TOMMY HANDLEY	Yes, in the morning. And go and get my rhetoric rompers and spouting suit.
F/X	**KNOCK ON DOOR**

TOMMY HANDLEY	Come in —
F/X	**DOOR OPENS**
MAN (Fred Yule)	Mr Handley — you remember me, don't you?
TOMMY HANDLEY	No, I don't think so Mr Heep. Who the dickens are you?
MAN	Don't you recollect when you were Mayor here, we used to work hand in glove?
TOMMY HANDLEY	Only when we were opening safes. You were Town Treasurer — when did you come out?
MAN	Oh, I got a pardon.
TOMMY HANDLEY	Eh?
MAN	Pardon.
TOMMY HANDLEY	I didn't hear anything. What do you want?
MAN	Well, we want you to take charge of all our V-day revels —
TOMMY HANDLEY	Now you're talking. We'll start a flag racket. Now go out and get me three thousand penny flags and sell them at ten-and-six each.
MAN	Isn't that black market?
TOMMY HANDLEY	No, red, white, and blue market —
MAN	You'll make a small fortune.
TOMMY HANDLEY	I'll make a big one. You know, a friend of mine in Oxford Street started with a tray of studs and finished with a string of race horses.
MAN	There'll be a small percentage for me of course?
TOMMY HANDLEY	How dare you. I'll call a policeman.
SAM	There's one outside boss —
TOMMY HANDLEY	Oh, I see. Well, er, how much do you want?
MAN	Fifty-fifty?
TOMMY HANDLEY	That's right —

F/X	**DOOR CLOSES**
TOMMY HANDLEY	This is a big idea, Sam. I'll show them how to celebrate V-Day. I'll have a red hot Variety Show, starting with Lupino Flame and finishing with Issy Bonfires
SAM	Who's going to produce it, boss?
TOMMY HANDLEY	John Fireman. We'll make a packet Sam. Now first of all go out and double the price of everything. I'll organise the celebrations. Now what should we have first?
F/X	**DOOR OPENS**
COLONEL CHINSTRAP (Jack Train)	A large brandy, sir —
TOMMY HANDLEY	It's old Beer Gynt — are you still celebrating Colonel?
COLONEL	I've celebrated every victory since Mafeking, sir.
TOMMY HANDLEY	By the look of your face you must have started with William the Pub Crawler.
COLONEL	There is only one thing I deeply regret, sir.
TOMMY HANDLEY	What's that? That you haven't got a reserve tank?
COLONEL	No, sir. That on this glorious occasion they should close *any* of the public hou any of the time.
TOMMY HANDLEY	I agree, but you can close all of the pubs all of the time gentlemen please —
COLONEL	How do you think I'm looking these days, sir?
TOMMY HANDLEY	Well I can't make up me mind whether you're floodlit or bloodshot.
COLONEL	I'm slightly shot sir, but never flooded —
TOMMY HANDLEY	Oh, by the way, Colonel. I've just been appointed Master of the Revels.
COLONEL	Ah, now you're talking sir. I say, why not put me in charge of the refreshments?
TOMMY HANDLEY	No fear — last time you made the tea with boiling gin instead of water and afterwards everybody had forty tiddley winks . . . All right Colonel, you organise the drinks and I'll relieve you now and again.
COLONEL	Oh thank you, sir. By gad sir, I'll do my duty. *(sings)* Hi! Hi! Clear the way — here comes the galloping Colonel!

F/X	**DOOR CLOSES**
TOMMY HANDLEY	That's very funny, he didn't have a drink off me tonight. It must be the thin end of the pledge. Well, now, I must arrange about the music —
F/X	**DOOR OPENS**
Charles Shadwell	Did you say music Tommy?
TOMMY HANDLEY	Oh, it's Chas. You know when you stand up straight you look like 'I' Day.
Charles Shadwell	'I' Day?
OMNES	'I' Day!
Charles Shadwell	Talking about days —
TOMMY HANDLEY	Yes, Gert?
Charles Shadwell	I've got the very tune for you. 'Happy Days Are Here Again' arranged by Gordon Jacob.
TOMMY HANDLEY	Well I'd rather hear The End of All Germany's Dreams and the Little Red School House at Rheims arranged by Eisenhower, but play on Chas —
ORCHESTRA	**'HAPPY DAYS ARE HERE AGAIN'**
	(applause)
TOMMY HANDLEY	Now Sam, I'm going to put you in charge of the fireworks. You can look after the set piece.
SAM	She's outside boss —
TOMMY HANDLEY	I'm not talking about my permanent judy, I mean illuminated faces — you know, like the Colonel's —
SAM	But boss, pyrotechnical progress postulates a preliminary positioning of pseudo-political portraiture presuming that the proletariat prognosticates problematically —
TOMMY HANDLEY	Sam, would you like to repeat that with your trap shut?
SAM	O.K. boss *(repeats unintelligibly)*.
TOMMY HANDLEY	Now open the trap and let the dog out.
F/X	**DOOR OPENS**

Jean Capra	Excuse us, but my girl friend and I would like to help you with your party, wouldn't we, love?
Ann Rich	Och aye — we're gey fond of dancing and we're awfu' fond o' the lads.
TOMMY HANDLEY	I must get a word in somehow.
Ann Rich	Och, what are you haverin' for?
Ann & TOMMY	We've no time for blathering. We've got to give the boys a good time, haven't we, hen?
Jean & TOMMY	Yes, ever such a good time — we think you're ever such a sport.
Ann & TOMMY	Come away hen, the man's daft.
Jean & TOMMY	Yes, ever so —
F/X	**DOOR SHUTS**
SAM SCRAM	Boss, you were marvellous. However did you do it?
TOMMY HANDLEY	Do you want to know how it's done?
SAM & TOMMY	Yes boss — how's it done?
TOMMY HANDLEY	That's how it's done. Now try it on the piano.
F/X	**PHONE**
TOMMY HANDLEY	Hullo?
MAN FROM THE MINISTRY (Clarence Wright)	Mr Handley — I said Handley. What time do you start your celebrations — I said celebrations.
TOMMY HANDLEY	Eh?
MAN FROM THE MINISTRY	I said what time do you start the festivities — I said festivities.
TOMMY HANDLEY	Ah, that's a secret — I said it's advertised all over the place. We start at eight o'clock — I said 9.30 — I shouldn't be at all surprised.
MAN FROM THE MINISTRY	Can I have a free pass for my girl friend — I said friend.
TOMMY HANDLEY	No, you can't have a pass for your friend — I said is she nice?

MAN FROM THE MINISTRY	Yes, very — I said very.
TOMMY HANDLEY	Oh — I said K. Of course she can have a seat — I said on my lap.
MAN FROM THE MINISTRY	Well, toodle-oo — I said toodle-oo.
TOMMY HANDLEY	Well Waterloo — I said Paddington.
F/X	**PHONE RINGS OFF**
TOMMY HANDLEY	I haven't heard from him for a long time. I expect he's been on a holiday — I said jail —
F/X	**DOOR OPENS**
MRS MOPP (Dorothy Summers)	Can I do you now, sir?
TOMMY HANDLEY	Hello Mrs Mopp. Tell, me why are you standing on one leg?
MRS MOPP	Well sir —
TOMMY HANDLEY	Don't tell me — so it was you I saw posing as Eros in Piccadilly on Tuesday night?

MRS MOPP	Oh sir, I did enjoy meself. Every time I waved me flag I found meself on top of a taxi with a soldier.
TOMMY HANDLEY	Well you were lucky to get one. I came home by Underground — I slipped down a manhole and caught the last drain.
MRS MOPP	The sailors were a bit saucy. There was one kept bumping into me and calling me 'his little collision mat'. He fell for me in a big way, sir —
TOMMY HANDLEY	What? Did he jump off a lamp-post and land on your quarter deck? What about the R.A.F.?
MRS MOPP	Oh sir — what a flighty lot. Why they wanted me to do the Victory Roll —
TOMMY HANDLEY	Well, you shouldn't do your hair up in a bun — they thought you were a piece of cake. Anyway, Mrs Mopp, I want you to appear in my victory parade.
MRS MOPP	Not as Godiva, sir — I'm sure that's where I caught me rheumatism.
TOMMY HANDLEY	You must have sat on a damp horse . . . No, I want you to be Queen Elizabeth and I'll be Sir Walter Raleigh.
MRS MOPP	Really?
TOMMY HANDLEY	No — Rawley.
MRS MOPP	Oh sir, couldn't I be something romantic, like Grace Darling?
TOMMY HANDLEY	All right — you be Grace Darling and the Colonel can be the wreck. He won't need any rehearsing.
MRS MOPP	What are you going to be sir?
TOMMY HANDLEY	Oh, I'll put a burnt cake on my napper and go as King Alfred.
MRS MOPP	I brought this for you, sir.
TOMMY HANDLEY	Oh isn't that nice. What is it? A rubber rissole?
MRS MOPP	It's me V-Day offering sir — I call it Peace Pudding.
TOMMY HANDLEY	I suppose when you stick your fork in it it sounds the last 'all clear'.
MRS MOPP	Oh sir. Well —T.T.F.N.
TOMMY HANDLEY	Hip-hip-hooray —
Sydney Keith	(neighs)

MRS MOPP	What's that, sir?
TOMMY HANDLEY	Three cheers for Winnie!
F/X	**DOOR CLOSES**
TOMMY HANDLEY	Victory's gone to her head, I'm afraid — she's never been the same since Gladstone chose her as Miss 1888.
SAM SCRAM	Boss, there's a man outside with a hat called Billy.
TOMMY HANDLEY	Well, ask him the name of his overcoat and I'll see him.
SAM	And boss, there's a deputation here to see you —
TOMMY HANDLEY	I'll see them one at a time.
F/X	**DOOR OPENS**
SAM	This way sir —
TOMMY HANDLEY	Ah! *There* you are —
WHATS'ISNAME (Horace Percival)	Eh?
TOMMY HANDLEY	No — I said ah.
WHATS'ISNAME	Oh!
TOMMY HANDLEY	Oh, so it's you is it? You seem to pop up everywhere. Won't you tell me who you . . .
WHATS'ISNAME	Ahhh!
TOMMY HANDLEY	*There* you are!
WHATS'ISNAME	I'm the chair . . . chair . . .
TOMMY HANDLEY	Well, I'm the table — all we want is the sofa and we're furnished.
WHATS'ISNAME	Oh, I don't mean that. No, no, no, I mean I'm, I'm, I'm the chairman of the com . . . com . . .
TOMMY HANDLEY	Oh, come, come!
WHATS'ISNAME	No, no, no, no. Itee . . .

TOMMY HANDLEY	Itee?
WHATS'ISNAME	Itee.
TOMMY HANDLEY	Isn't it a pity.
WHATS'ISNAME	Yes. No! No, I'm chairman of Foaming-at-the-Mouth V-Day Celebration Committee — er — er — don't you understand?
TOMMY HANDLEY	So you can talk, eh?
WHATS'ISNAME	Ah —
TOMMY HANDLEY	Now stop that. Who's going to be the guest of honour?
WHATS'ISNAME	You are.
TOMMY HANDLEY	*There* you are. You've got me at it now.
WHATS'ISNAME	Yes and we'd rather, er, rather —
TOMMY HANDLEY	Rather have a beer?
COLONEL CHINSTRAP	Good idea, sir. Make it three.
TOMMY HANDLEY	Oh, hop it Colonel. You know, I've got a lot of — a lot of the —
WHATS'ISNAME	Yes, too much.
TOMMY HANDLEY	Yes, yes, this is getting us . . . surely you know us . . . know us . . .
WHATS'ISNAME	Ark?
TOMMY HANDLEY	I'm listening. Well, to resume our interesting conversation sir — I'm sorry to keep you so . . . so . . .
WHATS'ISNAME	Long?
TOMMY HANDLEY	Ta-ta.
F/X	**DOOR CLOSES**
SAM SCRAM	What is the matter with him boss?
TOMMY HANDLEY	Ah . . .
SAM	*There* you are —

TOMMY HANDLEY	Don't you start that. I wonder why the committee's up against me . . .
F/X	**DOOR OPENS**
Clarence Wright	They've tumbled to you — *(maniacal laugh)* —
TOMMY HANDLEY	Hey, come here a minute. Charlie —
Charles Shadwell	Yes?
TOMMY HANDLEY	Listen to this. Do that again, will you?
Clarence Wright	*(laughs)*
TOMMY HANDLEY	What do you think of that Charles?
Charles Shadwell	Oh bother!
F/X	**DOOR CLOSES**
TOMMY HANDLEY	That's upset Chas. He's afraid he'll have to stick to music now.
F/X	**BUZZER**
MISS HOTCHKISS (Diana Morrison)	Mr Handley —
TOMMY HANDLEY	I thought the war was over.
MISS HOTCHKISS	Mr Handley!
TOMMY HANDLEY	Surrendering!
F/X	**DOOR OPENS**
MISS HOTCHKISS	Mr Handley — I trust today that you've got a certain amount of dignity and decorum?
TOMMY HANDLEY	Well, I've got two-penn'orth of dignity but they wanted points for decorum.
MISS HOTCHKISS	I mean, do not besmirch the reputation of the Empire.
TOMMY HANDLEY	It wasn't me — I couldn't get in.
MISS HOTCHKISS	Are you entirely brainless or deliberately obstructive?
TOMMY HANDLEY	Yes. Come on, let's be human —

MISS HOTCHKISS	No!
TOMMY HANDLEY	Then I'll be a little monkey. Lend me a flea, will you?
MISS HOTCHKISS	Can't you understand that I want you to behave yourself?
TOMMY HANDLEY	All right, I'll use my loaf and behave very well-bred —
MISS HOTCHKISS	Doh!
TOMMY HANDLEY	Same thing!
F/X	**DOOR CLOSES**
TOMMY HANDLEY	Do you know every time I see that prune-like mole on her cheek I want to throw custard at it. Well now I must get on with this procession —
F/X	**DOOR OPENS**
SINGOR SO–SO (Dino Galvani)	Mr Tom Francisco, I am invictoriated —
TOMMY HANDLEY	You mean D-Day lighted. I want you to look after the music.
SO–SO	Ah — that is a job after my own harp.
TOMMY HANDLEY	Harp? Are you the harp that once or twice — you know all about music, eh?
SO–SO	Of music I am a regular cycling Ophelia. I know every nut —

MMY HANDLEY	Every nut? Ah – a pupil of Sir Adrian Boult.
SO–SO	Mr Handlebar, I studied at the Royal Macademy.
MMY HANDLEY	Macademy? That was a hard road. I bet you came out top of the concert pitch.
SO–SO	I know more about music than Sir Thomas Beechead, or Basil Caramel.
MMY HANDLEY	How about John Barberpoley and York Hamburg? I'm glad you're an expert because I've hired a barrel organ for you.
SO–SO	Oh, I cannot play a thing like that. I should feel a silly fool – a proper nanny.
MMY HANDLEY	Nanny?
NANNY (Diana Morrison)	Yes, Master Tom.
MMY HANDLEY	Not you, nurse. Put me down.

SO–SO	No, no. My fellow musicians will say I have let down my profusion.
MMY HANDLEY	Well, you can always tie it up with a blue ribbon. Now come, So-So, put your earrings on and play it.
SO–SO	Oh botherino.
MMY HANDLEY	Oh, Mother Riley.
F/X	**BARREL ORGAN**
Ann Rich	Hello Tommy. That was smashing. Can I sing about it?
MMY HANDLEY	Hello Ann. What *is* the song?
Ann Rich	It's the 'Barrel Organ Rhapsody', Tommy.

TOMMY HANDLEY	Right. Well, I'll hold the handle and you do the turn.
ANN RICH & **ORCHESTRA**	**'BARREL ORGAN RHAPSODY'**
	(applause)
SAM'SCRAM	Boss, there's another deputation to see you.
TOMMY HANDLEY	Who are they? Animal, vegetable or neutral?
SAM	I don't know boss. But they speak a funny language.
TOMMY HANDLEY	A funny language — a new race of comedians. Patagonia . . . Well, send them in.
SAM	This way gentlemen . . .
F/X	**DOOR OPENS**
TOMMY HANDLEY	Ah, good morning gentlemen. Now, what can I do for you?
MEN	*(gibberish, on the theme of 'Vorjack')*
TOMMY HANDLEY	All right. One at a time, please now — you sound like four bulls arguing the toss. Who's the interpreter?
Horace Percival	Vorjack.
TOMMY HANDLEY	All right, Joe, Now sir, you with the astrakan boot laces, what have you got to say?
Clarence Wright	Vorjack — Vorjack — Vorjack . . .
TOMMY HANDLEY	Interpreter — what did he say?
Horace Percival	Vorjack.
TOMMY HANDLEY	Well that's fair enough. Now sir, you with the straw trousers and the tin tit for tat, what have you got to say?
Fred Yule	*(deep)*Vorjack — Vorjack — Vorjack.
TOMMY HANDLEY	Interpreter, what did he say?
Horace Percival	Vorjack.

TOMMY HANDLEY	Ah, now I can see nightlight. Now sir, you wearing the white nightie and tea cosy, what's your opinion?
Jack Train	Hmm . . . Vorjack.
TOMMY HANDLEY	Vorjack. Well thank you, gentlemen. Now we're all agreed on that — *(double talk)* — not forgetting the *(more double talk)* . . . Interpreter, tell them what I said.
Horace Percival	He say 'Vorjack'.
Fred Yule	Vorjack.
Clarence Wright	Vorjack.
Jack Train	Vorjack.
TOMMY HANDLEY	Oh, —four jack! Well, I've got four aces so I take the kitty. Show 'em out, Sam.
SAM	Where shall I put 'em boss?
TOMMY HANDLEY	In the Vorjack.
F/X	**DOOR CLOSES**
TOMMY HANDLEY	Well that's the best of a good education. I'm glad I went to Oxford and stayed the night . . .
F/X	**DOOR OPENS**
SAM	Boss, the procession's ready to start.
TOMMY HANDLEY	Let's have a look. Who are all the little girls in white? Brownies?
SAM	Boss, look at all those Kentucky Minstrels with white feet —
TOMMY HANDLEY	Kentucky . . . Don't be silly. Those are Bevin boys, they've just been paddling. Now tell the band to strike up.
SAM	Which song boss?
TOMMY HANDLEY	Our Victory Song, dedicated to the man who's won the war.
SAM	You, boss?
TOMMY HANDLEY	Well that's very loyal of you Sam, but I smoke a pipe. Now start the procession.

ORCHESTRA	MUSIC UP AND UNDER
TOMMY HANDLEY	We're glad we walked behind the man who smoked the big cigar –
OMNES	Tra-la-la-la, tra-la-la-la, tra-la-la-la-la-la.
TOMMY HANDLEY	We'd follow the man whose master plan has carried us through the war –
OMNES	Tra-la-la-la, tra-la-la-la, tra-la-la-la-la-la.
TOMMY HANDLEY	One sniff of the Old Havana – We'd follow him right to Fugiyama, We're glad we walked behind the man who smoked the big cigar –
ORCHESTRA	MUSIC UP
OMNES	Tra-la-la-la, tra-la-la-la, tra-la-la-la-la-la.
	(drum beat and applause)
TOMMY HANDLEY	Which way do we go Sam?
SAM	Left boss.
TOMMY HANDLEY	Right Sam.
ORCHESTRA	MUSIC UP AND UNDER
TOMMY HANDLEY	We're glad we walked behind the man who smoked the big cigar –
OMNES	Tra-la-la-la, tra-la-la-la, tra-la-la-la-la-la.
TOMMY HANDLEY	We'd follow the man whose master plan has carried us through the war –
OMNES	Tra-la-la-la, tra-la-la-la, tra-la-la-la-la-la.
TOMMY & Jean	One sniff of the old Havana – We'd follow him right to Fugiyama –
TOMMY HANDLEY	We're glad we walked behind the man who smoked the big cigar – Tra-la-la-la, tra-la-la-la, tra-la-la-la-la-la. Lumme Sam, where's the procession?
SAM	They've gone the other way boss.
TOMMY HANDLEY	We must have gone down the wrong street. *(sniffs)* I can smell chips – we're all right, they've gone down the wrong street.
MAN (Fred Yule)	Oh Mr Handley. I'm from the BBC *(laughs)* – they've sent me out with this microphone to ask how V-Day affects you. Would you say a few words?

TOMMY HANDLEY	Certainly. Ladies and gentlemen.
MAN	Excuse me. *This* is the microphone — *that* is a lamp-post.
TOMMY HANDLEY	Oh, sorry. Just force of habit, you know.
MAN	Not at all. Now, will you say something Mr Handley?
TOMMY HANDLEY	Right — Vorjack. Here, give me that mike, I'll ask the questions. Now sir, will you say a few words?
ALI OOP	Excuse please, mister.
TOMMY HANDLEY	Lumme, it's Ali Oop.
ALI OOP	Mister, you buy saucy flag — made of rag —
TOMMY HANDLEY	Don't hang carpets on the mike.
ALI OOP	Oh mister — you like funny pictures — private life of Boadicea — very rummy, oh lumme.
TOMMY HANDLEY	Give them to me. Why they're not fit to be seen. Sam, get them enlarged. Go away, Ali, we're broadcasting.
ALI OOP	All right, all right, all right. I go — I come back.
TOMMY HANDLEY	Now sir, I'm collecting opinions of V-Day. What's yours?
COLONEL CHINSTRAP	Anything that's left sir.
TOMMY HANDLEY	Good heavens, the Colonel's still standing. Go away old boy. Now madam, would you like to speak down the mike —
POPPY POOPAH (Jean Capra)	Well I don't know I'm sure — *(giggles)* —
TOMMY HANDLEY	Go on, you never know, Leonard Urry might be listening. What's your name?
POPPY POOPAH	Bubbles Brown —
TOMMY HANDLEY	That's funny, so do mine. What's your address?
POPPY POOPAH	22 Acacia Road.
TOMMY HANDLEY	Thank you.
POPPY POOPAH	Will I be hearing from you?

TOMMY HANDLEY	Yes, I'll be round just after nine. You've got the address down, Sam?
SAM	Yeah boss.
TOMMY HANDLEY	How big's your father?
POPPY POOPAH	Oh, he's huge.
TOMMY HANDLEY	Rub it out Sam. Anybody else? Ah, this is interesting, a bearded baby in a three-wheeled pram smoking a clay pipe. What did you do on V-Day Sonny?
MARK TIME (Jack Train)	I'll have to ask me Dad –
TOMMY HANDLEY	I'm getting sick of this. Is there anyone here with a mind of their own?
MISS HOTCHKISS	Mr Handley!
TOMMY HANDLEY	That's torn it, Sam. Quick, behind this water tank. We must get *somebody* to say *something*.
F/X	**KNOCKING**
TOMMY HANDLEY	Who's that knocking on the tank?
THE DIVER	Don't forget the diver, sir – don't forget the diver.
TOMMY HANDLEY	Lumme, it's Deepend Dan. Listen, as the war's over, what are you doing?
THE DIVER	I'm going down now, sir.
F/X	**BUBBLES**
TOMMY HANDLEY	Well that concludes our broadcast 'Static at the Corner' – back to the studio. How do we get there Sam?
SAM	Follow the band boss.
TOMMY HANDLEY	Oh of course, that's an idea. Come on everybody –
ORCHESTRA	**MUSIC UP AND UNDER FOR 'THE MAN WITH THE BIG CIGAR' TO FINISH**

With the end of the war came the end of a chapter in ITMA's history. Some 170 programmes had been broadcast during wartime, and the show had become the longest-running comedy half-hour on radio. In particular, the six series in the previous four years had provided a rich and steady diet of radio characterization. Week after week, Tommy Handley had been surrounded by his affectionate, sometimes cheeky, but always loyal friends—generous Mrs Mopp, the ultra-polite duo of Cecil and Claude, leering Ali Oop, Signor So-So, excitable Sam Scram and his pal Lefty, the Commercial Traveller, the thirsty Colonel. Situations changed, other characters came and went, but the core had remained the same.

The triumvirate behind the shows decided that the time had come for a change of both characters and scene, for to continue as before was to invite boredom among an audience which was now spread across two hemispheres. Handley's capers had always taken place in England, and it was agreed that the first series of peacetime programmes should be set in a kind of never-never-land, a faraway country whose inhabitants could poke gentle fun at events at home. The choice was a distant, recently discovered island which was annexed to the Empire: Tommy was to be Governor there, and it was fittingly christened 'Tomtopia'.

During the summer break in 1945, Francis Worsley, Ted Kavanagh, and Tommy Handley tackled the difficult job of re-casting. Dorothy Summers, Sydney Keith, Horace Percival, and Dino Galvani left, while Jack Train, Fred Yule, Diana Morrison, and Jean Capra stayed on. These four were joined by Clarence Wright, who had returned after his tour, Carleton Hobbs, Hugh Morton, Mary O'Farrell, Michele de Lys, and Lind Joyce, ITMA's singer for the next three years. Towards the end of the series Charles Shadwell would take his own band out on tour, and Rae Jenkins would step in to conduct.

It was in the first programme of the series that the move to Tomtopia was announced. There followed two weeks of preparation, and then a month's sea journey to get there. The time on the ship provided Ted Kavanagh with his first opportunity to create a collection of new characters. The passengers' meals were prepared by Chef Curly Kale (Carleton Hobbs), a character who was sickened by the thought of food but revelled in the old and well-worn jokes which he told Handley every week. A direct opposite, Fred Yule's George Gorge could eat untold quantities of 'lovely grub', and made listeners' mouths water at a time when rationing was still a condition of their lives. Hugh Morton created Sam Fairfechan, the Welshman who on his first meeting with Handley revealed the characteristic which was to remain with him through two series: seeing the Governor-to-be peering down into the ship's engine room he remarked, 'Come down by all means—I have taken the ladder away.' Other travellers included Nurse Riff-Rafferty (Mary O'Farrell), Tommy's old nanny who had crystal clear recall of the rogue as a child and an abundance of her own earthy memories, coy Lady Sonely (Mary O'Farrell), and Carleton Hobbs' nameless character, whose weekly banal tales were introduced and concluded with 'Ain't it a shame, eh? Ain't it a shame.'

The ship reached Tomtopia towards the end of October, and Handley was greeted on arrival by both the natives and the resident, though small, English colony. Diana Morrison, who had been ill during the beginning of the series, was there to deliver Hotchkiss' own commanding welcome. The native chief was polygamous Bigga Banga (Fred Yule), whose language was a gibberish called Utopi; his daughter Banjeleo (Lind Joyce) knew a smattering of English and served as interpreter. Another notable native was Hugh Morton's Wamba M'Boojah, his Oxbridge accent the result of a spell as a BBC Overseas Service announcer during the war. The English colony included Major Munday (Carleton Hobbs), who had moved to the island shortly after the Boer War and firmly believed in the continuing existence of a nineteenth-century England, and his daughter Naieve (Jean Capra), equally isolated and exceedingly ignorant. Stella Stalls arrived sometime before Christmas, determined to introduce culture to the island with her drama group.

Shortly after the two hundredth programme on 21 February 1946, a Government Commission descended on the island, sent by Whitehall to examine the running of the colony. This sequence of programmes inspired an ITMA friend to give a Tomtopian lunch at London's Connaught Rooms in June, complete with jungle decor and a menu designed by Mendoza. After lunch, prominent civil servants, lawyers, educators, etc. humorously lambasted every aspect of Tomtopian life.

Listeners accepted the new ITMA setting, and catchphrases were once again sought after and repeated. Some favourite elements in the programmes were the L-infested remarks of Bowing and Scraping (Jack Train and Hugh Morton), the shrill call of 'no cups outside' by Ruby Rockcake, tea lady at the railway buffet (Mary O'Farrell), and the reminiscent conversations between Major Munday and Colonel Chinstrap (who had accompanied Tommy to the island and headed straight for the Jungle Arms on arrival) about their coincidental time together in India. From the positive response to this new, peacetime series it was clear that That Man, who had achieved an unprecedented success during the war, was to continue at the top.

Deryck Guyler

Alias
Dan Dungeon
Sir Short Supply
Percy Palaver
Frisby Dyke

Remembers

I remember ITMA best for the marvellous degree of teamwork which existed among all those involved. It was wonderful to work with Tommy Handley, and his warmth and good nature provided the atmosphere in which friendliness and cooperation flourished.

Tommy was an unselfish artiste, always willing to help, equally pleased when others got the laughs. I had come to ITMA in 1946 with a drama background, a complete newcomer to the light entertainment field. I was, naturally enough, very nervous about my first performance, and the presence of an audience added to my fears. As my turn came and I neared the microphone, Tommy moved to the side to leave me centred on the mike—a rare thing to do for a new artiste, but very much like his generous self.

Among the first parts I played were Percy Palaver, the governor of Tomtopia installed in Tommy's absence who mumbled most of the time, punctuated his 'speech' with 'Oomyahs' and 'Hrrrumphs', and was very rarely intelligible, and Sir Short Supply—a ministerial character who had a soft spot for Hotchkiss.

Best-known among my roles was Frisby Dyke, the Liverpudlian and sometime seeker after knowledge. Frisby was unique, for it was the first time that a Liverpool accent had ever been used in any areas of entertainment. Tommy always used to ask his mum for advice for she was, of course, an avid listener. She was also very shrewd, and gave excellent tips on which characters to keep and which to lose. After Frisby had been in the series for six weeks or so, Tommy went home for a weekend and asked his mother what she thought about Frisby Dyke. 'He's very funny—gets lots of laughs,' came the response. 'Yes, but what do you think about the accent?' 'Accent?' his mother replied. 'There's no such thing — you must be daft.' Although Liverpudlians were the only ones who knew what it all meant, they would deny to the end that they had an identifiable 'accent'.

The name of the character was an accident. One night during a programme Tommy looked at me and said, 'Why there's my old friend, Frisby Dyke.' This caused a bit of an uproar because that was the name of an old Victorian store in Liverpool and there was a strict BBC injunction against anything approaching advertising. The store, however, had been blitzed during the war, and the name stuck. Despite unlikely names, ITMA characters often became real to the listeners in a way which, perhaps, only radio can foster. I once got a letter—or rather Frisby Dyke did —from an old vicar somewhere in the country. He was writing because he had one Captain Dyke buried in his cemetery, and wondered if he were any relation!

Tommy Handley was a great personal friend during those few years before his death. We had the common interests of Liverpool—he used to say we had put it on the map together—and criminology. Tommy had a scrapbook full of trials from Crippen onwards, and many of his friends were barristers and judges—who would often come to the shows. If he had a fortnight free, he'd spend it at the Old Bailey. When Tommy died, it was almost as if we'd lost a member of the family.

As a broadcaster, his personality had come across on the air as well as another's might on the Palladium stage. The qualities which rang through again and again were those of warmth and sincerity, qualities which had kept up the morale of the nation during the war. I well remember one letter which Tommy had received from a Tank Commander who had been in the desert during the Alamein campaign. His tank had been cut off from all the others, and the crew couldn't get its bearings at all. While trying to make contact on the radio, they tuned into ITMA. The entire crew sat and listened for the whole half hour before getting on with the business of finding out where they were—a rare kind of tribute indeed.

Above, Jack Train and Hugh Morton demonstrate Bowing and Scraping; *above right*, Fred Yule with a mid-morning snack for George Gorge; *right*, Hugh Morton's Sam Fairfechan: 'I hope you live to a ripe old age!'; *below*, Handley, Worsley, and Kavanagh reach a unanimous decision at a script conference!

Tommy Handley
in
It's That Man Again

(No. 17 Ninth series—No. 194)
Transmission
Thursday, 10th January 1946, 8.30-9.00 p.m.
Home Service

ANNOUNCER	This is the BBC Home Service — ITMA!
ORCHESTRA	**FANFARE LEADING INTO SIGNATURE TUNE**
OMNES	It's that man again, Yes, that man again, Yes sir, Governor Handley is here —
BOWING (Jack Train)	Last week you heard him called Dada —
SCRAPING (Hugh Morton)	Which made Miss Hotchkiss angly —
BOWING & SCRAPING	Ha-ha!
OMNES	Mother's pride and joy, Mrs Handley's boy, Oh, it's useless to complain — When trouble's brewing, it's his doing, That man, that man again!
LADY SONELY (Mary O'Farrell)	Ah — my dear Miss Hotchkiss — my dear, dear Miss Hotchkiss. You lucky girl to have come in for all that money last week —
MISS HOTCHKISS (Diana Morrison)	Lady Sonely, I have *no* money. That vulgar rumour was circulated by Governor Handley. Why, he even proposed marriage to me.
LADY SONELY	*(laughing)* Oh, how ridiculous!

MISS HOTCHKISS	I beg your pardon? What *is* ridiculous is to see you fawning upon him —
LADY SONELY	Miss Hotchkiss, how dare you! I shall inform the Colonial Office. *(fuming off)* I've never been so insulted —
F/X	**DOOR CLOSES**
MISS HOTCHKISS	Oh, this is disgraceful — where is he? Good gracious, there he is. Look what he's doing — I suppose he calls that educating the natives!
TOMMY HANDLEY	I'll pay pontoons only — Hello folks!
	(applause)
	And hello Hotch — what are you doing with a face as long as Issy Bonn's top note?
MISS HOTCHKISS	What do you mean by spreading the tale that I had come into money?
TOMMY HANDLEY	Well, you shouldn't wear mink corsets and a banana skin coat.
MISS HOTCHKISS	You even offered to put a ring on my finger —
TOMMY HANDLEY	Well, I couldn't get at your big toe. You'd got your boots on —
MISS HOTCHKISS	I'm impervious to further insults from a stupid nincompoop —
TOMMY HANDLEY	Are you suggesting that I'm nincompoopus mentis? I shall sue you for steak and kidney porpoise —
MISS HOTCHKISS	What are you talking about?
TOMMY HANDLEY	The Law — everything you say will be taken down, mended and put on again. Talking like that — coming the sulphuric with me. Who do you think you are, the head prefect? Lend us half a dollar — come on.
MISS HOTCHKISS	There is *no* money in the Treasury — you owe everybody.
TOMMY HANDLEY	And you owe me something, too —
MISS HOTCHKISS	What do I owe you?
TOMMY HANDLEY	A penny – I'm not going down to the station with you again — always spending my money on platform tickets.
MISS HOTCHKISS	Doh!
F/X	**DOOR CLOSES**

TOMMY HANDLEY	Money, money. What is money? Filthy lucre. And what's filthy lucre? A dirty old tramp peeping through a telescope. Now where can I get some?
F/X	**DOOR OPENS**
MAN (Clarence Wright)	I say —
TOMMY HANDLEY	Yes?
MAN	Just a minute — have a look at this paper.
TOMMY HANDLEY	Hullo — it's that delicious rotter again.
MAN	Have a look in the Agony Column — what's it say?
TOMMY HANDLEY	Well, it says, 'Gold mine for sale — nearly new. Or would exchange for a flat in Golder's Green. Apply: Chief Wamba M'Boojah, Carleton House Kraal, Elephant's Walk'. This sounds a bargain —
MAN	You should buy it, y'know. Do yourself a bit of good.
TOMMY HANDLEY	Gold mine, eh? I wonder what kind it is — a pin-up table in Piccadilly or a drug store near a dog track —
MAN	No, no. It's a real gold mine. A real one. Get in on the ground floor —
TOMMY HANDLEY	Right — you leave the pantry window open and I'll have a go.
MAN	That's the boy.
F/X	**DOOR CLOSES**
TOMMY HANDLEY	He's a nice chap, that. Joined the Army on Monday and came out on Tuesday with six blankets and two demob suits. Now I'll go down and have a look at this mine. Hey, rickshaw!
BOWING	Solly, no more pletrol —
SCRAPING	Gloing back to bleakfast?
BOWING & SCRAPING	Ha-ha!
TOMMY HANDLEY	Oh, it's you two again, eh? Now cut out that taxi patter and take that kimona off your flag — I want to see Chief Wamba M'Boojah.
BOWING	Solly, taxi broken down.
SCRAPING	No go.

BOWING & SCRAPING	Ha-ha!
TOMMY HANDLEY	Haul it away then.
BOWING	O.K.
BOWING & SCRAPING	*(singing to 'Volga')* Ha-ha, ha-*ha*, ha-ha, ha-*ha*, ha-ha.—
TOMMY HANDLEY	You know, those two sat under Ernie Bevin's table at the state banquet last night and sang 'You know and I know but what do we care'. Hullo, there's a man cleaning his suede shoes with a porcupine. Can I help you, sir?
MAN (Carleton Hobbs)	Ain't it a shame, eh? Ain't it a shame?
TOMMY HANDLEY	Oh, it's you, is it? What's today's great big shame?
MAN	I waited for hours in a fish queue, and I got a nice bit of filleted, and then the man behind me said 'Go outside and see if it's raining', and when I came back he'd taken my plaice. Ain't it a shame, eh? Ain't it a shame?
TOMMY HANDLEY	He adores fish, that fellow — why he even puts on a walrus moustache and joins the seals at feeding time. You ought to see him catch a herring with his hands behind his back. Well, it's time I got a spurt on —
F/X	**DOOR OPENS**
COLONEL CHINSTRAP (Jack Train)	A Burton, Handley? Excellent beer — I'll have a pint.
TOMMY HANDLEY	Hello, Colonel. Tell me, are you smoking a fox's tail or is your tongue hanging out?
COLONEL	No sir — a frightful thing's happened. I've suddenly become addicted to water.
TOMMY HANDLEY	Well, that's terrible — our living's gone now and who's going to feed the pink elephants.
COLONEL	Don't despair, sir. Water never harms anyone, provided it is taken in the right spirit.
TOMMY HANDLEY	That's better. Spoken like a sozzler and a gentleman. But tell me, Colonel, between these four pubs, have you ever really tasted water?
COLONEL	It was once administered to me, sir. You see, I fainted —
TOMMY HANDLEY	Was that the time you saw Red Snakes in the Sunset?

COLONEL	No sir. It was the day my watch stopped and I arrived just as they were closing —
TOMMY HANDLEY	And I suppose you pushed into the pub, paused, and passed out?
COLONEL	It's funny you should say that, sir. In the 1st Foot and Mouth we never went on manoeuvres without a tot or two —
TOMMY HANDLEY	What, the Aldershot Otterto or Oxshot and Bagshot Ottertatoo. Well, run along now, Colonel, and buy a tot for me.
COLONEL	*(singing)* Oh, I ain't got a barrel of money Don't think I'm trying to be funny —
TOMMY HANDLEY	We'll have one for the road, With Campbell and Joad,
BOTH	Side by side.
F/X	**DOOR CLOSES**
TOMMY HANDLEY	Now, I must get on the track of this gold mine — this looks like the Chief Wamba's bungalow. Yes, it's got a board outside — 'Alvar M'Boojah, ex-BBC Announcer. "A cough, a wait, an apology." The Frank Phillips of the jungle. Stuart Hibberd says, "Cor lumme, what a lovely larynx".' I'll see if he's in.
F/X	**KNOCK, THEN DOOR OPENS**
TOMMY HANDLEY	Ah, good morning M'Boojah.
WAMBA M'BOOJAH (Hugh Morton)	Call me Alvar, Handley old man. After all, we're old BBC School chums.

TOMMY HANDLEY	Yes, but I was expelled for taking off my trousers and putting on records. Now what about this gold mine you advertised? Is there much in it?
M'BOOJAH	Oh, oodles, I believe. But diggin' is rather a dirty business, y'know.
TOMMY HANDLEY	I don't know. I had some very nice clean digs in Sheffield — even the canary used a serviette. How much do you want for it?
M'BOOJAH	Well, as a matter of fact, old man, I'll let you have it for a plastic pullover — I think they're positively smashing.
TOMMY HANDLEY	Well, I'm out of those at the moment, but I could do you a nice line in slender gents' palm leaves, guaranteed caterpillar proof. It's a deal then, the mine's mine?
M'BOOJAH	Absolutely, old top. You'll find gold mining most awfully really frightfully exhilarating.
TOMMY HANDLEY	I'm glad. I haven't had a thrill since I went to the Hippodrome Nuremberg and saw Goering flying in 'Peter Pan'.
M'BOOJAH	Well, bung frightfully ho, old fruit —
TOMMY HANDLEY	Well, spin frightfully fast, old top —
F/X	**DOOR CLOSES**
TOMMY HANDLEY	You know, he wasn't very popular at the BBC — he used to make them all feel so common. Now, I'd better find someone who knows something about gold mining.
F/X	**DOOR OPENS**
1ST BOY (Jean Capra)	Here, Tommy, Miss Hotchkiss says we've got to work in your perishing pit —
2ND BOY (Lind Joyce)	I'm not going down any blinking coal mine —
TOMMY HANDLEY	Coal mine? It's a perishing gold blinking mine. Now listen, boys. Come in with me, and you'll be rich beyond the dreams of Hammersmith.
BOTH	Coo-er!
TOMMY HANDLEY	Yes, you can have anything you want — a sack full of ice cream, a stuffing full of dolly mixtures, a solid gold football —
2ND BOY	Garn, you're kidding. What are you going to have?
TOMMY HANDLEY	I'll have a cigar a mile long, a box of matches, and a girl in slacks to strike 'em on — Now you buzz off and get down the mine.

1ST BOY	No, you go down the mine, Daddy!
TOMMY HANDLEY	Daddy! Get out of here!
F/X	**DOOR CLOSES**
TOMMY HANDLEY	What a pair they are — in and out of Dartmoor as if they owned the place! Now, I must get picking. Ah, there's a signpost pointing the way.
Charles Shadwell	I'm not pointing, Tommy.
TOMMY HANDLEY	Why it's Chas! Chas, you want to be rich? All you've got to do is to buy a share in my gold mine —
Charles Shadwell	How much?
TOMMY HANDLEY	Well, let me see now, you'll want five hundred shilling shares at one and sixpence, entertainment tax, thirty pounds, preferential follirollicle eight and three-quarters, less corkage, that brings the total to two hundred and ninety pounds, sixteen shillings and ten pence — plus debentures.
Charles Shadwell	Too much.
TOMMY HANDLEY	All right. I'll take away the debentures.
Charles Shadwell	What happens then?
TOMMY HANDLEY	The people have to sit on the grass. What are you going to play?
Charles Shadwell	I've got the very thing — George Melachrino's monetary masterpiece called 'Tales from the Bretton Woods'.
TOMMY HANDLEY	Or, 'Alone, We Did It'. Well, play, Chas —
ORCHESTRA	**'TALES FROM THE BRETTON WOODS'**
	(applause)
TOMMY HANDLEY	I'll bet they enjoyed that in Thugmorton Street. Wait till I return to England a millionaire — I'll buy a tobacconist shop, lock the door, wait till there's a big queue and blow all the smoke through the keyhole. Now I'd better get digging.
F/X	**DOOR OPENS**
MAN (Fred Yule)	Hmm — excuse me —
TOMMY HANDLEY	What, have you done it again? What do you want?

MAN	Well, I've got the very thing here for you — something that no rich man should be without.
TOMMY HANDLEY	What is it? A chorus girl?
MAN	No, a bottle of 'Phew' the offensive ink.
TOMMY HANDLEY	Offensive ink? What do I do with it — write rude words on the walls?
MAN	No, no, no. It's for answering begging letters. It only writes three words — 'Dear Sir, No.'
TOMMY HANDLEY	Let me try it —
MAN	Here you are.
F/X	SCRATCHING
TOMMY HANDLEY	Why that's no good to me.
MAN	Why not?
TOMMY HANDLEY	Well, look what it's written — 'Dear Madam, Yes.'
MAN	Oh, bother!
F/X	DOOR CLOSES
TOMMY HANDLEY	How dare he! Offensive ink — trying to get me to blot my copybook. Now where's that miner I engaged to help me?
F/X	DOOR OPENS
SAM FAIRFECHAN (Hugh Morton)	Good morning. Here I am. Whatever made me come?
TOMMY HANDLEY	Hello, Sam. I'm delighted to see you. Come in — I've gone away for the weekend.
SAM	So you need an expert miner. I know the very man for you — it is my old woman.
TOMMY HANDLEY	Your old woman — what does she do besides fill the sink and wash your back? Have you been underground before?
SAM	Oh, I was underground for five years — standing up all the time on my stomac
TOMMY HANDLEY	Oh, of course, you had the bunk below me at Bond Street Tube Station. Many's the fag-end I've dropped in your mouth when you've been snoring.

SAM	I am looking forward very much to working in the mine. Nothing will ever get me down.
TOMMY HANDLEY	Oh, have you ever tried hitting Joe Louis? Now off you go, get down the mine and don't forget to blow your candle out when you get to the bottom.
SAM	I have a special safety lamp, it is absolutely foolproof. You light it, count five and off it goes — bang.
F/X	**DOOR CLOSES**
TOMMY HANDLEY	Now I must get my things together. *(singing to tune of 'Mairsy Doats')* Davy Lamps and lumps of gold, my dinner in my hanky — a kettle of Irish stew, lovely brew. Oh, pickled pork and cheddar cheese, oh where's my blinking pick axe? —
F/X	**DOOR OPENS**
MAN (Clarence Wright)	Just a minute — there's no gold in the mine at all.
TOMMY HANDLEY	No gold? Well, I'll eat eighteen carrots. Lumme, now there won't half be a bullion and cow —
MAN	It's all right. I'm going to plant a gold brick there. You find it and all the women will be after you.
TOMMY HANDLEY	Then I'll be able to take down a bird in a gilded cage — what a lark, eh?
MAN	That's the boy!
F/X	**DOOR CLOSES**
TOMMY HANDLEY	What a charming criminal type he is — lovely close-set eyes and sloping forehead. I bet he gets into Parliament as soon as he picks the lock.
F/X	**DOOR OPENS**
NAIEVE (Jean Capra)	Can I see you, Your Excellency?
TOMMY HANDLEY	Of course you can Naieve — I'm just inside this shirt. What's the trouble?
NAIEVE	My father wants to send me to a finishing school in England —
TOMMY HANDLEY	What? All the way to England to find out how much it costs to buy nothing? My dear girl, put yourself in my hands. Why, I used to lecture in a girls' school - on conkology.

NAIEVE	What's that?
TOMMY HANDLEY	Er — the study of noses. It wouldn't interest you.
NAIEVE	Why?
TOMMY HANDLEY	Ay, there's the snub —
NAIEVE	Did Miss Hotchkiss have to learn about noses?
TOMMY HANDLEY	Her — why, she was on the front row when they were given out. I used to superintend the games, too.
NAIEVE	What games?
TOMMY HANDLEY	You're right. What games they were. I remember once nailing a pancake to the tail of the headmaster's shirt. I'll never — well anyway, you don't want to leave Tomtopia, do you, now that I've bought a gold mine?
NAIEVE	What is a mine?
TOMMY HANDLEY	Well, it's a thing you go down.
NAIEVE	Why?
TOMMY HANDLEY	Well, because it's so nice when you come up again — and gold is a kind of solid custard that you can't pour on rhubarb you know. Anything else?
F/X	**DOOR OPENS**
MAJOR MUNDAY (Carleton Hobbs)	Ah, my dear boy. I hear you've discovered gold on the island. When I heard the news from my old friend, Bigga Banga, I said 'Eureka!'.
TOMMY HANDLEY	So did I the first time he came near me. He was furious, he was — his face went as black as a sheet.
MAJOR	Now run along, Naieve — I want to speak to His Excellency about the mines.
COLONEL CHINSTRAP	Mine's a large whiskey.
TOMMY HANDLEY	I'll join you, Colonel — give me a large pot of glue.
MAJOR	Ah, good day to you, Chinstrap.
COLONEL	Good day, sir. Do you remember, Munday, when we were in Liverybad? That night in the mess I sat next to a young Ensign —
TOMMY HANDLEY	'Enson? Don't tell me Leslie's baby's taken to the bottle?

MAJOR	I remember him — Crumborne Carstairs, wasn't it?
COLONEL	Yes, poor old Crummy — he made an awful gaffe.
TOMMY HANDLEY	We didn't haff laff.
MAJOR & COLONEL	Silence, civilian!
TOMMY HANDLEY	Bah, tenders —

COLONEL	Yes, he dipped his cigar in melted butter and tried to smoke his asparagus — rather revolting, Handley.
TOMMY HANDLEY	Oh, I don't know. I sat next to Gordon Richards at the Jockey Club dinner when he suddenly said 'We're off', jumped on a saddle of mutton, put a bit in his mouth and whipped the cream — any objections?
COLONEL	By the way, Munday, have you heard that Income Tax in England is going to be reduced?
MAJOR	And about time, too — eightpence in the pound. Ruination!
F/X	**DOOR CLOSES**
TOMMY HANDLEY	Eightpence in the pound. He ought to be in England now that April's near. I wonder if that gold brick's been planted yet?
F/X	**DOOR OPENS**
LADY SONELY	Ah, my dear Governor — I hear that everything you touch turns to gold.
TOMMY HANDLEY	That's right, Lady Sonely. Only this morning I touched the Colonel and he instantly turned into a bar.
LADY SONELY	I've heard all about your wonderful discovery — I want to have *three* shares. Here is my money, the widow's mite.

TOMMY HANDLEY	Ah, but some widows might not. I remember when I was she-ing at Little Bispham I met one . . . Well, tell me, how many shares would you like?
LADY SONELY	I'll take three shilling ones.
TOMMY HANDLEY	Just a minute — I'll get my brokers on the phone.
F/X	**TELEPHONE**
TOMMY HANDLEY	Is that Threadneedle, Thimble and Darn It? Is that Mr Wool?
WOOL (Hugh Morton)	Wool speaking.
TOMMY HANDLEY	Oh, hello Wool, you old worsted. I rang you about my high percentage stock — how's it going?
WOOL	Going up nicely.
TOMMY HANDLEY	What price are they now?
WOOL	Sixpence a bunch.
TOMMY HANDLEY	Sixpence a bunch — my high-priced percentage stock?
WOOL	Oh. I thought you said night-scented stock *(laughs off)* —
F/X	**TELEPHONE RINGS OFF**
LADY SONELY	Well, Your Excellency, how much are the shilling shares now?
TOMMY HANDLEY	Sixpence a bunch — I mean three pounds, ten shillings. Goodbye, Lady Sonely.
LADY SONELY	Goodbye, you dear, dear man *(laughs off)* —
F/X	**DOOR CLOSES**
TOMMY HANDLEY	Things are going swimmingly as the man said when he was hit on the head with a mallet. 'Ullo, who's this girl with a silver spade dressed up like a night club navvy? Pardon me, fair one, are you after gold?
Lind Joyce	What do you think, big boy — I've been a gold digger all my life.
TOMMY HANDLEY	So that's why you left England suddenly, eh? Guilty conscience.
Lind Joyce	Who do you think you are, anyway?
TOMMY HANDLEY	I'm nobody — I'm just a guy that owns a gold mine.

Lind Joyce	Gold mine! Darling! I love gold.
LIND JOYCE & ORCHESTRA	**I'M GOING BACK ON THE GOLD STANDARD'**

(applause)

TOMMY HANDLEY	What a lovely girl — what a gorgeous head of bootlaces. Now I really must get mining.
F/X	**DOOR OPENS**
CURLY KALE (Carleton Hobbs)	Good evening, sir.
TOMMY HANDLEY	Oh hello, Curly. What's the trouble?
CURLY	I've had an accident with the bread, sir.
TOMMY HANDLEY	Oh. Did you leave your teeth in the crust?
CURLY	No sir. But I couldn't get yeast, so I used liver salts and it's all come out in a rash.
TOMMY HANDLEY	Well, sell it as red currant bread. You'd better tell me one of your funny stories to take the taste away.
CURLY	This is a snorter, sir. *(quickly)* A man kept a sow in his back yard and the other day she had a lot of little pigs. A neighbour called and said, 'Can I see the little swine?' and the man's wife said, 'He's not in — he's gone to the pictures'. Do you like that?
TOMMY HANDLEY	That's a silly story — they don't allow pigs at the pictures. Off you go, Curly tail — Kale.
F/X	**DOOR CLOSES**
TOMMY HANDLEY	He must be Nat Gubbins of Tomtopia.
F/X	**DOOR OPENS**

MAN (Clarence Wright)	I say — just a minute. It's started — they're all running.
TOMMY HANDLEY	I don't care. I'm not lending my hanky to anybody.
MAN	No — the Gold Rush. They're flocking to the place.
TOMMY HANDLEY	Did you plant the gold brick?
MAN	No, I couldn't get any gold paint. But it doesn't matter — the money's flowin
TOMMY HANDLEY	But they must find something. I know, plant this diamond and gold tie-pin that Carroll Levis gave me when he discovered me in Tessie O'Shea's dressing room.
MAN	That's the boy!
F/X	**DOOR CLOSES**
TOMMY HANDLEY	What a rat he'd make for Dick Whittington —
F/X	**BICYCLE BELL**
TOMMY HANDLEY	Lumme, here's Hotchkiss coming along on a bamboo bike, with a Chinese lantern hanging on her nose. Miss Hotchkiss!

MISS HOTCHKISS	Peddling!
TOMMY HANDLEY	I see that. Just a minute, what a lovely saddle-bag you've got at the back.
MISS HOTCHKISS	That is my cycling costume.

TOMMY HANDLEY	What a bloomer — you shouldn't come out in those.
MISS HOTCHKISS	Why not?
TOMMY HANDLEY	Well, you'll have all the kids chasing you and shouting 'Take 'em off — we know you!'
MISS HOTCHKISS	Thomas!
TOMMY HANDLEY	Foxglove. *(pause)* Do you remember that night when we first met?
MISS HOTCHKISS	No. Where was it?
TOMMY HANDLEY	I don't know. I remember you wore a locket with a picture of Joe Becket in it.
MISS HOTCHKISS	No — it was in your office.
TOMMY HANDLEY	Oh yes. And we had to have tea in the safe because the man was coming to take the cup back. How about coming into permanent partnership with me?
MISS HOTCHKISS	You mean?
TOMMY HANDLEY	I do — buy ten thousand shares in my gold mine and we'll both go to prison together. Doh — I've said it for you. Ta-ta.
F/X	**DOOR CLOSES**
TOMMY HANDLEY	I'm glad I said 'Doh' first — it took the bread right out of her mouth. Where is that mine?
F/X	**DOOR OPENS. VOICES UP**
TOMMY HANDLEY	Oh, I say. Gosh — the gold rush has started all right. I've never seen so many people since the local butcher put a man in his window with a notice 'Horses queue up here'. Now what's Chief Bigga Banga saying to the crowd?
BIGGA BANGA (Fred Yule)	*(Utopi)*
	(razz)
TOMMY HANDLEY	He's getting the blackbird —
	(Utopi)
	(renewed cries)
TOMMY HANDLEY	What did he say?

BANJELEO (Lind Joyce)	He say your friend say the gold is underneath his pumpkins.
TOMMY HANDLEY	That's a bit awkward.
BIGGA BANGA	*(Utopi)*
TOMMY HANDLEY	Gosh, he's getting bitter.
COLONEL CHINSTRAP	A bitter, sir. I don't mind if —
TOMMY HANDLEY	Colonel, get Bigga out of here. He's queering my pitch.
COLONEL	Right sir. I say, Bigga — *(Utopi)*
BIGGA BANGA	*(Utopi)*
COLONEL	*(Utopi)*
BIGGA BANGA	*(Utopi)*

COLONEL	There you are, Handley. What do you think? He's drinking out of my hands. We're going round to the Jungle Arms.
TOMMY HANDLEY	Thank you, Colonel. And don't forget if he winks at the barmaid he's not getting fresh — he's getting hungry.
COLONEL	Certainly, sir. Come, chief — *(exit speaking Utopi).*
MAN (Clarence Wright)	I say — just a minute. They've dug up that tie-pin of yours and sent it to be analysed.
TOMMY HANDLEY	You couldn't have fairer than that — gold *and* diamonds in one mine.
MAN	I'll go along and hear the result. See you later.
TOMMY HANDLEY	Hullo — there's another crowd. What's going on?

STELLA STALLS	If money be your God, give ear —
MMY HANDLEY	She means give it 'ere. Lumme, it's Stella Stalls doing a Lillian Braithwaite into a megaphone.
STELLA STALLS	Give your money to Art — to Art.
MMY HANDLEY	Who's he?
STELLA STALLS	Art. Contribute to my National Theatre — a Temple of Thespis.
F/X	**HEN NOISES**
STELLA STALLS	Ooh!
MMY HANDLEY	Lumme, what a wealthy country this is — they throw hens instead of eggs.
STELLA STALLS	Begone, knave, and let me speak on —
MMY HANDLEY	*(singing)* Speak on the begone — bring on the baboon — Ladies and gentlemen, let me speak. Untold wealth lies beneath yonder pumpkin patch.
MAN (Carleton Hobbs)	Yonder what?
MMY HANDLEY	Patchkin pump — hmm — ken pump patch — er — I'll start again. Under the spreading chest pump catch — the village pump katch kins — anyway, there's gold there. All I require from you is enough money to get a doss down for the night.
MAN (Clarence Wright)	I say — just a minute. Here's the public analyst. He's examined your gold and diamond tie-pin — we're in the money.
MMY HANDLEY	Good. And now Mr Public Anagrammaticist, what have you found — gold *and* diamonds.
ANALYST (Fred Yule)	*(North country)* Gold and diamonds — hee, hee — nay, it were brass and glass.
MMY HANDLEY	Brass and glass!
BOTH	Aye, brass and glass.
MISS HOTCHKISS	Mr Handley!
MMY HANDLEY	Ba guming!
ORCHESTRA	**SIGNATURE TUNE TO FINISH**

At the end of the ninth series Governor Handley had left Tomtopia and sailed for England. He felt that the island setting could survive another year's programmes, and Ted Kavanagh and Francis Worsley agreed. During the summer months there were some more additions to the cast: Molly Weir (at one time the fastest typist in Britain at 300 words per minute), well known in Scotland but new to English audiences, Joan Harben, an accomplished actress who had not worked in radio before, and Deryck Guyler, for whom it was a first venture into light entertainment. Jean Capra left, and Diana Morrison would take time off during the series to have a baby.

There was, at the time, a lot of talk about projects to send a rocket to the Moon, and the 1946 Ideal Homes Exhibition had exhibited a model projectile. The beginning of the tenth series was set at Castle Weehouse, somewhere in Scotland, with Tommy trying to organise a flight to the Moon. Molly Weir became Tattie Mackintosh, the perky Scots lass who was the bane of Handley's existence. Deryck Guyler provided Dan Dungeon, the jokey castle guide, and Sir Short Supply of the Ministry of Food. Born in Wallasey, Cheshire, Guyler was already greeting Handley with 'Hey, whacker', though the immortal character of Frisby Dyke was to emerge in a later series. The Colonel's nephew appeared on the scene (Hugh Morton's Brigadier Dear), a young, teetotaling, military enthusiast who was shamed by his uncle's every action, and Joan Harben created Mona Lott, the gloomy laundrywoman who delivered her tales of woe in the flattest and most melancholy of cockney voices, but always insisted that it was 'being so cheerful as keeps me going'.

The rocket was launched at the end of October, missed the Moon, and landed on Tomtopia. A new Governor had been installed in Tommy's absence, and the rivalry between the inarticulate Sir Percy Palaver (Deryck Guyler) and Handley continued throughout the series, All the old Tomtopian friends were there, together with the man who spoke in Spoonerisms (Hugh Morton) and Joan Harben's fast-talking, opinionated woman, who paused only to bark 'Down Upsey' at her yapping little dog.

At the end of this series, Handley, Kavanagh, and Worsley spent some time in

America, a visit which combined a holiday with a look at American radio and would provide them with a freshness of approach on their return.

The first programme of the next series, in autumn 1947, appropriately opened with Handley's return from the United States. He was immediately directed to the Labour Exchange, where he was told that he was to be the Government's adviser on industrial and scientific affairs. His various tasks during the series included taking a look at the radio industry, engineering a fuel saving campaign, investigating industrial psychology, and organising a PR programme for England. Hattie Jacques had joined the cast and with her came Sophie Tuckshop, the schoolgirl who dreamt of marzipan pillows and ate as richly, combatting the ill-effects of her diet with a giggle and 'but I'm all right now'. A much-admired interlude in these programmes was the weekly conversation between Handley and Frisby Dyke, a Liverpudlian dialogue on words from which Frisby always emerged triumphant. Other additions were Fred Yule's Atlas ('What me? In my state of health?') and the man who began every conversation in a whisper and ended in a deafening shout (Hugh Morton).

A high point of the series was a visit by the Royal Family to the BBC. The occasion was the Silver Jubilee celebrations, and ITMA was chosen as the example of radio variety. The theme of the programme, which was televised, was a tour of Broadcasting House, and the script was full of Royal references. After the performance the ITMA team was presented to the King and Queen.

The series which began in October 1948 saw Tommy Handley somewhat down on his luck. A permanent resident of Henry Hall, the tramps' guest house run by Miss Hotchkiss, he floated from job to job—a situation which gave Ted Kavanagh scope to poke fun at virtually any British institution. On 28 October, ITMA had its three hundredth birthday. Assigned to a job at Madame Tussaud's, That Man stumbled across a door marked 'The Hall of ITMA's Past'. Accompanied by the Colonel, he went through to find a reunion of his friends from Foaming-at-the-Mouth and Tomtopia, a birthday celebration which delighted both Handley and his audience.

Hattie Jacques

Alias
Ellie Phant
Sophie Tuckshop

Remembers

I believe I was the last person to join the ITMA team—a very young and inexperienced radio performer, and starry-eyed about working with Tommy Handley. How I ever passed the audition, I don't know—I was so nervous that Tommy held my hand to stop it from shaking.

I remember I was given a copy of *Picture Post*, opened at random, and Tommy and Francis Worsley told me to read the article in as many different accents as I could, changing every two sentences or so. It turned out to be an article full of statistics about the paddy fields in China! I can't tell you what a mess I got into—a sort of Stanley Unwin delivery, with a Japanese-Welsh or French-Irish accent. Tommy laughed so much I got the giggles, and found myself with the job.

It was planned that I should play a character named 'Ella Phant'. Ted thought the laughs would come on the size gags but, being radio, and coupled with the fact that my voice didn't have the timbre of a 'heavy', that didn't really work out. It wasn't until one show when Tommy was supposed to be passing through a department store and knocked over a speaking doll (me) that the audience reacted favourably. A large lady with a very little voice seemed to hit the spot, so 'Sophie Tuckshop' was born—the terrible child who never stopped eating, with inevitable sickening results.

I shall never stop being grateful for the opportunity of working with Tommy, who must have been one of the greatest radio performers we have ever known. I learned (I hope) so much from him. His timing was unerring, his generosity as a performer unlimited, and his warmth a quality the whole nation was aware of, as was evident at his funeral—

the streets were lined with people unashamedly crying at the loss of a dear friend.

All of us who worked with him loved him, and he loved and cared for us. He enriched our lives in every way, and I am proud to have been in his company.

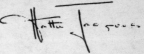

Top, Mona Lott (Joan Harben) recites her tale of woe for Tommy, as the rest of the cast and the BBC Variety Orchestra listen in.

Above right, Frisby Dyke (Deryck Guyler) and Handley clash over words; *above left*, Lind Joyce, Tommy Handley, and Hattie Jacques.

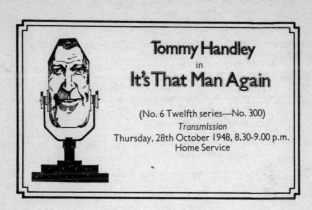

Tommy Handley

in

It's That Man Again

(No. 6 Twelfth series—No. 300)
Transmission
Thursday, 28th October 1948, 8.30-9.00 p.m.
Home Service

ANNOUNCER	This is the BBC Home service —
SOPHIE TUCKSHOP (Hattie Jacques)	Oh, Mummy, is it true that Mr Handley has been on the air for three hundred years?
MRS TUCKSHOP (Joan Harben)	Don't be silly dear. It only *seems* like three hundred years. Actually, it's a case of —
ANNOUNCER	Ladies and gentlemen, for the 300th time — ITMA.
ORCHESTRA	**FANFARE LEADING INTO SIGNATURE TUNE**
OMNES	It's that man again, Yes, that man again, Yes sir, Tommy Handley is here —
MEN	Sing 'Happy Days' and 'Auld Lang Syne' He's been that man since one nine three nine —
WOMEN	May Mrs Handley's son In the years to come His gaiety retain,
OMNES	At ninety-three may he still be That man, that man again!
F/X	**PHONE**

MISS HOTCHKISS (Diana Morrison)	Good morning. Yes, this is The Hall. Yes, Henry Hall — The Tramps' Guest House. Matron speaking. Yes, I have the very man. You want him right away Good morning. *(rings off)* *(shouts)* Warden. Send in Number 300 — Handley, T.
WARDEN (Fred Yule)	If I can find him. Has he packed up that building job?
MISS HOTCHKISS	He lasted one day.
WARDEN	Lumme — a record! I'll try and track him down, Miss.
F/X	**DOOR CLOSES**
MISS HOTCHKISS	What a sad thing it is. Poor Mr Handley — after all I've tried to do for him and where has it got him?
F/X	**TIN WHISTLE: 'CONQUERING HERO'**
MISS HOTCHKISS	Good heavens.
F/X	**WINDOW UP**
MISS HOTCHKISS	That's him standing in the gutter. Mr Handley — why are you playing a tin whistle?
TOMMY HANDLEY	Well, I've got the wrong shaped legs for a cello — Hello folks!
	(applause)
	For an encore I will play a Russian military new step entitled 'The Army of today's all Left'.
MISS HOTCHKISS	Mr Handley — come in here at once.
TOMMY HANDLEY	Ah — the voice of the Turtle. All right ducks!
F/λ	**DOOR OPENS AND CLOSES**
TOMMY HANDLEY	Good morning Hotch. What's on the Agenda today, and no vetoes.
MISS HOTCHKISS	Mr Handley, last week you placed me in an awkward position.
TOMMY HANDLEY	I'm sorry, Hotch — I locked the wrong door. Never mind, I'll turn over a new leaf, as the model said to the sculptor — Now what is this job?
MISS HOTCHKISS	Nightwatchman at the Waxworks.
TOMMY HANDLEY	Waxnightman at the Watchworks! What — me, spend all night with Crippen and Stuart Macpherson? Not blinking likely.

140

MISS HOTCHKISS	Now take this card and go to the Waxworks and report at the door marked 'Push'. Got that?
TOMMY HANDLEY	Which door?
MISS HOTCHKISS	The door marked 'Push' — understand?
TOMMY HANDLEY	Yes. *(sings)* I must report at the door marked 'Push', The door marked 'Push', The door marked 'Push'. I must report at the door marked 'Push', And not at the door marked 'Pull'. Then I'll go to the door marked —
MISS HOTCHKISS	Rubbish!
TOMMY HANDLEY	Door marked 'Rubbish', Door marked 'Rubbish' —
MISS HOTCHKISS	Mr Handley — will you be serious?
TOMMY HANDLEY	I am serious and what's more as I sit through the long watches of the night, I shall pretend you're there among the wax figures of famous women.
MISS HOTCHKISS	Oh, Thomas, and what will you do?
TOMMY HANDLEY	I'll put an arm round your waist and a hot water bottle down your back.
MISS HOTCHKISS	Hot water bottle?
TOMMY HANDLEY	Yes — then you'll either melt in my arms or run away under the door.
MISS HOTCHKISS	Doh!
F/X	**DOOR OPENS AND CLOSES**
TOMMY HANDLEY	Nightwatchman at a Waxworks. What fun I'll have — I'll go up to the 'Brides in the Bath' and let the water out and then I'll glue a moustache on Lady Godiva's horse. That'll give them something to talk about. Well, I must get going now.
F/X	**DOOR OPENS. TRAFFIC NOISE**
TOMMY HANDLEY	What a wonderful day for buying 150 candles twice. Now, I wonder what bus I should take. Oh, pardon me Inspector — what bus for the Waxworks?
INSPECTOR (Hugh Morton)	*(whispering)* I'm sorry. I don't know.
TOMMY HANDLEY	Which way do they go?

INSPECTOR	I'm sorry, I don't know.
TOMMY HANDLEY	They seem to go every way, don't they?
INSPECTOR	Yes — that makes it worse.
TOMMY HANDLEY	Why are you speaking like that? Have you lost your voice?
INSPECTOR	No!
TOMMY HANDLEY	Then why are you talking in a whisper?
INSPECTOR	I don't want them to know —
TOMMY HANDLEY	To know what?
INSPECTOR	That I've LOST MY SENSE OF DIRECTION!
F/X	**BUS NOISES UP**
TOMMY HANDLEY	Lost his sense of direction, eh? Why don't they make him Minister of Labour. Now — I'll just take a chance. Ah, here's a bus coming — I wonder if this goes to Marylebone.
F/X	**BUS PULLS UP**
TOMMY HANDLEY	Hey, Conductor, where does this bus go to?
CONDUCTOR (Deryck Guyler)	Clricklewood, Willesdlen, Golder's Gleen and Holloway —
TOMMY HANDLEY	I beg your pardon?
CONDUCTOR	I said we go to Clricklewood, Willesdlen, Golder's Gleen and Holloway.
TOMMY HANDLEY	I wish you'd rinse that sago pudding out of your mouth and tell me if this bus goes to *(with l's)* Marylebone.
CONDUCTOR	Eh?
TOMMY HANDLEY	I said does this bus go to *(with l's)* Marylebone?
CONDUCTOR	*(with l's)* Now who's got sago pudding in his mouth? Listen, for Marylebone you want a trolley bus number 11.
TOMMY HANDLEY	*(with l's)* The number 11 trolley bus.
CONDUCTOR	Yes.
TOMMY HANDLEY	Well, thanks a million.

F/X	**BELL RINGS AND BUS GOES OFF**
TOMMY HANDLEY	Well, I'll have to walk. Which way to the Waxworks, Madam?
WOMAN (Joan Harben)	Disgraceful. A great big hulking brute like you wasting your time at the Waxworks.
TOMMY HANDLEY	But madam —
WOMAN	In the middle of the production drive, too.
F/X	**DOG BARKS**
WOMAN	Down Upsey!
TOMMY HANDLEY	Well, if it isn't my old friend —
WOMAN	Things have got to such a pitch that we married women will all have to work, and if I have to go, what do you imagine my poor husband will do?
F/X	**DOG BARKS**
TOMMY HANDLEY	Drown Upsey . . . Fancy meeting her — she hasn't changed much. The dog seems older, though. I'm sure he's suffering from fallen pads. Well, now I must look for the door marked 'Push'. Ah, this is it —
F/X	**DOOR IS PUSHED OPEN**
TOMMY HANDLEY	And here we are. Hello, what's this group? King John signing the Magna Carta at Runnymede.
COLONEL CHINSTRAP (Jack Train)	Rum and mead, sir? I don't mind if I do.
TOMMY HANDLEY	Hello, Colonel. What are you doing gazing at that figure of Bonnie Prince Charlie? He's not the man who invented whiskey.
COLONEL	Then he's no right here, sir.
TOMMY HANDLEY	Well, if it comes to that — what are you doing here?
COLONEL	Well sir, I thought of a way of getting a drink without Creep knowing — I come to the Waxworks, go down to the Chamber of Horrors, faint with fear and get a drop of brandy on the house.
TOMMY HANDLEY	Have you tried it?
COLONEL	Yes sir, but it didn't work.
TOMMY HANDLEY	Why not?

COLONEL	Well you see every time I fell down, an interfering attendant picked me up, dusted me, and said 'The mice have been at his feet again'.
TOMMY HANDLEY	Well, you'd better not let Creep catch you at it.
JOSIAH CREEP (Hugh Morton)	Little does he know that I'm here disguised as a sleeping beauty *(laughs)*.
TOMMY HANDLEY	Well Colonel, this is more in your line. 'The Sleeping Beauty' — just put a penny in and she becomes the heaving Judy.
COLONEL	I'm afraid I haven't got a penny, sir. We'll try this crown cork.
TOMMY HANDLEY	Crown cork! I'll put in the penny — I'll put it in.
F/X	**PENNY DROPS**
TOMMY HANDLEY	There you are. She's waking up — look, her mouth is opening — she's going to say something.
F/X	**WHIRRING SOUND, THEN GIRL'S VOICE: WOODPECKER'S SONG**
TOMMY HANDLEY	Lumme — it's the *Creeping* Beauty. I didn't know Creep was married. There's something rum about this place.
COLONEL	Rum, sir? I think I'll go and find out where it is. Good day, sir *(makes a quick exit)*.
F/X	**DOOR CLOSES**
TOMMY HANDLEY	Good day, Colonel. Well he went out as quick as a common informer who's just heard of a Sunday Variety show —

OLD WOMAN (Joan Harben)	Young man!
TOMMY HANDLEY	Eh?
OLD WOMAN	Could you tell me if the figures are — er — completely clothed?
TOMMY HANDLEY	How d'you mean?
OLD WOMAN	I mean do they in addition to their exterior attire — do they — I mean — underneath?
TOMMY HANDLEY	Oh yes, yes, of course, we change 'em every week — we've got to.
OLD WOMAN	Got to?
TOMMY HANDLEY	Yes, last week we found that Richard Coeur de Lion had got so rusty underneath that when we lifted up his arms, down came his tin trunks.
OLD WOMAN	Oh, thank you —
TOMMY HANDLEY	Not at all, you dirty old woman. Go away. Well this is interesting — now look at the tableau there. Queen Bess and Raleigh offering his cloak. I wonder what he's saying to her?
Hugh Morton	*(as Raleigh)* Now, now, don't dilly-dally. Give us that cloak — the cleaners close at six o'clock. Come, come . . .
TOMMY HANDLEY	Really, Charlie. Come-come Raleigh. Now, what can this group represent? It's marked 'The Burghers of Calais'. Well I'm not arguing.
MAN (Fred Yule)	You will have your little joke, Mr Handley. We're the choir *(sings scale with Tommy).*
TOMMY HANDLEY	I thought you were going to do that. But what are you doing here?
MAN	Well, as this is such a great day for you, we thought we'd serenade you and the other great figures of the past.
TOMMY HANDLEY	Eh? All right. Well, get going —
CHOIR & ORCHESTRA	'FOR HE'S A JOLLY GOOD FELLOW'
	(applause)
TOMMY HANDLEY	Well that's cleared everybody out. Now I'll have a good look round — Ah, the British Cabinet, 1888. Look at that old man with an Eton collar on upside down. Why it's Gladstone. Now I wonder what it was he said in 1888?

MAN (Jack Train)	Here cock — could you do with a pair of soskins?
TOMMY HANDLEY	Eh? Oh, it's you again is it? What are you doing in the Waxworks?
MAN	I work this joint. How about a dozen finnicky pins?
TOMMY HANDLEY	Finnicky pins?
MAN	Yes — they smell like kwangos, only more so.
TOMMY HANDLEY	Kwangos?
MAN	Yes, and I'll tell you what — I'll chuck in a dozen flamboys.
TOMMY HANDLEY	He's at it again — I must put a stop to this. You haven't by any chance got a few frog benders?
MAN	Frog benders?
TOMMY HANDLEY	Yes, you know. They've got mottrams on the dizzydays.
MAN	I don't get you, guv.
TOMMY HANDLEY	You're no use — go down and see Chilman at the Canny.
MAN	Canny?
TOMMY HANDLEY	Of course he can — he's always doing it. Now hop it. Trying to catch me — the man who caught measles when you couldn't get them for love or money. Ah, another old friend — King Alfred. Why, someone's pinched his cakes. I wonder who it was?
SOPHIE TUCKSHOP	It was me. *(giggles)* Hello.
TOMMY HANDLEY	Why, Sophie Tuckshop. Fancy, you're even eating waxcakes now —
SOPHIE	Well, only one.
TOMMY HANDLEY	Only one, eh? Well, how did you keep it down?
SOPHIE	I didn't — but I'm all right now. Would you like a sausage roll?
TOMMY HANDLEY	No thank you — I've just had lunch with a Scotty.
SOPHIE	Ooh — did you have haggis?
TOMMY HANDLEY	No, just a handful of biscuits and a rubber bone — but I'm all right now. I suppose you came here to study history. Who's your favourite character?
SOPHIE	Henry VIII. He ate such a lot, *and* with his fingers.

TOMMY HANDLEY	Aren't you thinking of Charles Laughton? I bet you'd have liked to have lived in those days.
SOPHIE	Oh, yes — I'd have stood behind him and caught the bits he threw away.
TOMMY HANDLEY	I see. *(sings)* Over his shoulder comes scrag end — Over his shoulder come dumplings — Are you still there, Sophie?
SOPHIE	Yes. I had a lovely dream last night — I dreamt the bed was made of marzipan and the mattress was marshmallow and the sheets were jelly and the pillows embroidered with lovely sugar violets . . . .
TOMMY HANDLEY	Stop! Once more we halt the roar of Sophie's Tuckshop to tell you of some of the interesting things that are In Tum Tonight! Carry on, Bicarb —
ORCHESTRA	MUSIC

TOMMY HANDLEY	Well, she's gone and by the look of it, only just in time.
OLD MAN (Hugh Morton)	Waiter! Bring me a pot of tea and *The Times.*
TOMMY HANDLEY	Pot of tea and *The Times?* What are you talking about?
OLD MAN	Go on, look sharp. I'll be in the Library.
TOMMY HANDLEY	Just a minute, chum —
OLD MAN	Chum? What is this place coming to? And that jockey, how did he get in? He's not a member.
TOMMY HANDLEY	A member? What are you talking about?
OLD MAN	This Club.
TOMMY HANDLEY	This isn't your Club. Can't you see that none of these figures are alive?
OLD MAN	Oh, it's the Athenaeum — my mistake. Wrong Club.
TOMMY HANDLEY	Oh pardon me, madam — what's at the bottom of these stairs?

MONA LOTT (Joan Harben)	The place where they make models of murderers, sir.
TOMMY HANDLEY	That's a familiar voice. Oh, it's you Mona. How did you get a job here?
MONA	Influence, sir — I've got a brother in the Chamber of Horrors.
TOMMY HANDLEY	Oh, a proper bad Lott — what's he in for? Singing 'The Woodpecker's Song'?
MONA	No sir — it's his job. He's the ticket collector.
TOMMY HANDLEY	Well, what made him choose this place?
MONA	Oh sir, he's always been keen on anything gruesome, sir. If there's one thing he likes of a Sunday it's a nice gory murder in the paper and pilchards in tomato sauce.
TOMMY HANDLEY	I'm different — all I want is bacon and bigamy. But what were you doing when I came in?
MONA	Just day dreaming, sir. You see, Little took me to the country last weekend. We had to stay the night in a bungalow with a leaky roof —
TOMMY HANDLEY	How awful.
MONA	Oh, it wasn't so bad, sir, until the tank in the attic burst and before we could say Robinson Crusoe the room was full of water —
TOMMY HANDLEY	Couldn't you have caught it in something?
MONA	No sir, everything was afloat including the bed.
TOMMY HANDLEY	Wasn't Little upset?
MONA	He was all right, sir. You see he got a bit merry coming down and when he saw me in the water he said, 'Lumme, Miranda the Mermaid,' and I had to sit on the what-not all night combing my hair.

TOMMY HANDLEY	Dear, dear. What happened next?
MONA	Well, Little started rowing the bed round the room shouting 'Any more for the Skylark?' and then somebody opened the bungalow door and he went sailing down the garden path and I haven't heard from him since.
TOMMY HANDLEY	Has Tom Arnold seen this production? Well Mona, what have you got to say about my 300th birthday?
MONA	Well sir, I made up a little poem for it. Shall I read it?
TOMMY HANDLEY	Please do, yes.
MONA	Right. Roses are red and violets are blue Excepting when it is snowing, But as I say it's being so Cheerful as keeps us going.
TOMMY HANDLEY	Thank you very much Mona Wheeler Wilcox — that was very charming.
MONA	You really think so, sir? You've made me so happy — *(exit crying).*
TOMMY HANDLEY	I've never been so touched, as the man said when his wife hit him on his anniversary with a flat iron. Ah well, now I'll go and bluff King Hal. Hello Bluff — you old scoundrel, marrying six wives. Why didn't you go on for the dozen?
ATLAS (Fred Yule)	What, me — in my state of health?
TOMMY HANDLEY	Atlas! What are you doing here all dressed up?
ATLAS	It's me new job. They've taken Henry VIII downstairs to have his eyes polished and I'm taking his place for a day.
TOMMY HANDLEY	How do you manage to stand so still — have they starched your tights?
ATLAS	No. Oh, but it's awful standing here for hours — I have to be so careful what I eat.
TOMMY HANDLEY	Well, judging by the look that Wolsey's giving you, you've been eating garlic. What's that big lump on your knee?
ATLAS	That's a pork pie that's slipped down.
TOMMY HANDLEY	Well, don't let the rolypoly get down the other leg or you'll be rumbled — and talking of rumbling how's the tummy these days?
ATLAS	Oh, my doctor says I'll have to nurse it.

TOMMY HANDLEY	You'll never find a cradle big enough to put it in. Besides, you'd want a choir to sing it to sleep. Well, so long Atlas, I must get on my way. Hold everything –
ATLAS	Oh dear –
TOMMY HANDLEY	Now I really will go into the Chamber of Horrors.
F/X	**CREAKING DOORS**
TOMMY HANDLEY	Good heavens – this is worse than I thought. Look at that brutal face with a mop of tousled hair. I wonder if he's ever committed murder?
Rae Jenkins	What, me – in my state of health?
TOMMY HANDLEY	Well – Rae the Ripper. Who or what are you and your cut-throats going to do today?
Rae Jenkins	Well, remembering all your old Itma friends, Ronald Hanmer has arranged 'Dear Old Pals' as a tribute to the whole Itma company, past and present.
TOMMY HANDLEY	That's a very long speech, Rae – has it left you any time for the music?
Rae Jenkins	Oh yes, Tom.
TOMMY HANDLEY	All right – 'Dear Old Pals'.
ORCHESTRA	**'DEAR OLD PALS'**
	(applause)
TOMMY HANDLEY	Rae, never in the whole of my three hundred Itma's have I heard such a piece of concentrated cacophony.
FRISBY DYKE (Deryck Guyler)	What's concentrated cacophony?

TOMMY HANDLEY	So I hit John Snagge in the eye with a handful of pease pudding and — eh? What did you say?
FRISBY DYKE	I said, what's concentrated cacophony?
TOMMY HANDLEY	Frisby, Frisby, Frisby — you come in here looking like the top of an old chutney bottle with the cork out and dare to interrupt me — and wrongly, too. You know, you want to watch your step or they'll keep you in here.
FRISBY DYKE	What — as a Waxwork?
TOMMY HANDLEY	Yes.
FRISBY DYKE	They can't do that — I've only got one suit.
TOMMY HANDLEY	They should have made a model of you as an awful example of congenital incapacity.
FRISBY DYKE	They wouldn't der.
TOMMY HANDLEY	What do you mean they wouldn't der?
FRISBY DYKE	They wouldn't der to put me in ther.
TOMMY HANDLEY	Why?

FRISBY DYKE	And anyway, if you can't explain one word why try and flummox me with another?
TOMMY HANDLEY	Would it be better if I called you a moronic ignoramus?
FRISBY DYKE	Oh, well, I don't mind that. The other one was a bit insulting, wasn't it?
TOMMY HANDLEY	Now listen, Frisby, this is an important day to me —
FRISBY DYKE	It's an important day for me, too.
TOMMY HANDLEY	Oh? Why?
FRISBY DYKE	Well, my sister's going into corduroy trousers — she likes the noise they make when she walks.

TOMMY HANDLEY	Noise? What sort of a noise?
FRISBY DYKE	Well it's a kind of concentrated cacophony.
TOMMY HANDLEY	That fellow Frisby's getting me down. I'll have to cut out the big words and use little ones —
COLONEL CHINSTRAP	A huge little one, sir — wonderful.
TOMMY HANDLEY	Hello, Colonel. I'm almost glad to see you. I've had a very trying day.
COLONEL	With me, sir, every day's a trying day.
TOMMY HANDLEY	Oh?
COLONEL	I'm always trying to get a drink. But for once I think I know where the bottle's buried — come with me, sir.
TOMMY HANDLEY	I certainly will, Colonel. Hello, here's a door I haven't been through for years — it's marked 'The Hall of Itma's Past'. Let's go in, Colonel, shall we?
F/X	**DOOR OPENS**
ORCHESTRA	**MUSIC**
TOMMY HANDLEY	Well, I seem to know all these figures — they look like old friends. My goodness they are old friends — my old pals of ten years' Itma. Oh, I know this one — black hat, black coat, and a white liver.
FUNF (Jack Train)	This is Funf speaking —
TOMMY HANDLEY	Well, I'll go back to Bristol.
ORCHESTRA	**MUSIC**
TOMMY HANDLEY	Strong smell of arsenic and old camels. You know, I've got a feeling that this is the point when somebody tries to sell me something.
ALI OOP (Horace Percival)	Excuse please, mister. You buy very saucy postcard? Very funny, oh lumme —
TOMMY HANDLEY	Why, it's old Ali Oop, still peddling along. No, I don't want anything today.
ALI OOP	No postcard, mister? Pity. All right. I go — I come back.
ORCHESTRA	**MUSIC**

F/X	**KNOCK ON DOOR**
TOMMY HANDLEY	Ah, another salesman, I bet.
F/X	**DOOR OPENS**
COMMERCIAL TRAVELLER (Clarence Wright)	Good morning.
TOMMY HANDLEY	Good morning.
TRAVELLER	*Nice* day.
TOMMY HANDLEY	No.
TRAVELLER	Any helicopters, motor cars or washing machines?
TOMMY HANDLEY	Yes, please.
TRAVELLER	You can't have them — they're only for export.
TOMMY HANDLEY	What have you come here for, then?
TRAVELLER	So that I can call again. Good morning.
TOMMY HANDLEY	Good morning.
TRAVELLER	*Nice* day.
F/X	**DOOR CLOSES**
ORCHESTRA	**MUSIC**
TOMMY HANDLEY	Ah, I recognize this guy with the earrings and the blond in an ice cream cart —
SIGNOR SO–SO (Dino Galvani)	Ah, Mr Handlebar. To see you I am delightful.
TOMMY HANDLEY	Signor So-So. Well, well, well. Tell me — how are things in Gorgonzola?
SIGNOR SO–SO	They are more than too good — they are not enough. But tonight I am as happy as a sandbag. Yes, this is the greatest movement of my life.
TOMMY HANDLEY	I see. Well, what have you been doing since I saw you last?
SIGNOR SO–SO	Notting at all. Notting at all.

153

ORCHESTRA	**MUSIC**
SAM FAIRFECHAN (Hugh Morton)	Good morning. How are you? — as if I cared.
TOMMY HANDLEY	Well, it's Sam Fairfechan, the biggest Aberystwyth in the world. What have you come for?
SAM FAIRFECHAN	I have come from my village in Wales and we all tell each other you're wonderful, but you can't believe a word we say —
ORCHESTRA	**MUSIC**
SAM SCRAM (Sydney Keith)	Hey, boss, boss. Sumpin' terrible's happened!
TOMMY HANDLEY	Sam Scram. Why Sam, you look as neat as an American food parcel. You do really. What's terrible?
SAM SCRAM	Well boss, the celebration of a centenary signifies the stupendous ceremonial splendiferousness of semi-sesquipedalian sensationalism —
TOMMY HANDLEY	Same patter — and same shirt. So long, Sam.
GRAMS	**DRUMS**
TOMMY HANDLEY	I say, it's come over dark. No it hasn't. It's a swarm of liquorice allsorts or something.
BIGGA BANGA (Fred Yule)	*(Utopi)*
TOMMY HANDLEY	Bigga Banga — with a new silk hat and beautifully creased legs. How are you, you old scoundrel?
BIGGA BANGA	*(more Utopi)*
TOMMY HANDLEY	Eh?
BANJELEO (Lind Joyce)	My papa he says, 'When do you come back to Tomtopia? Big Chief Income Tax wait for you.'
TOMMY HANDLEY	Thank you, Banjeleo. I think she looks charming with that bracelet round her ankle —
ORCHESTRA	**MUSIC**
MRS MOPP (Dorothy Summers)	Can I do you now, sir?

TOMMY HANDLEY	Dear old Mrs Mopp. Well, you do look well. You know, my dado has never been the same since you dusted it last —
MRS MOPP	I've brought this for you, sir.
TOMMY HANDLEY	Oh, isn't that nice. What is it?
MRS MOPP	It's a special birthday cake. Made out of me head.
TOMMY HANDLEY	I'll put a bonnet on before I eat it. Well, goodbye lovey.
MRS MOPP	T.T.F.N.
TOMMY HANDLEY	N.C.T.W.W.A.S.B.E.
MRS MOPP	What's that, sir?
TOMMY HANDLEY	Never clean the window with a soft-boiled egg. Well, it's nice to see all the old pals again.
OMNES	*(sing)* Dear old pals, jolly old pals, Clinging together in all sorts of weather — Dear old pals, jolly old pals —
TOMMY HANDLEY	Thank you everybody for your super-abundant spontaneity —
FRISBY DYKE	What's super-abundant spontaneity?
TOMMY HANDLEY	This is too much. This time you've had it, Fris — take that.
F/X	**BONK**
FRISBY DYKE	Ooh!
OMNES	*(sing)* Give me the friendship of dear old pals.
ORCHESTRA	**SIGNATURE TUNE TO FINISH**

There were to be only ten more broadcasts in the twelfth series. On 9 January 1949 Tommy Handley died suddenly of a cerebral haemorrhage. His death stunned a world-wide audience, many of whom had heard the repeat of the 310th programme just before the news came. From the tributes in the press and the letters from listeners, it was clear that people experienced a sense of personal bereavement. Thousands turned out to pay their respects on the day of the funeral, and again at the memorial services at St Paul's and Liverpool Cathedral.

Tommy Handley had lived his life with kindness, generosity, and respect for his fellow man. He had given freely of his leisure time, from his continuing interest in Boys' Clubs to charity appearances and local fêtes. By the time he died his fan mail had reached nearly one thousand letters a week, and he insisted on answering all of them personally, and by hand. In a very real sense, he gave his life to the people who loved him—members of a radio family in whose homes he had been a weekly guest for nearly ten years.

At the memorial service at St Paul's the then Bishop of London spoke for those thousands when he paid a final tribute to the man who had been ITMA: 'He was one whose genius transmuted the copper of our common experience into the gold of exquisite foolery. His raillery was without cynicism, and his satire without malice . . . From the highest to the lowest in the land people had found in his programme an escape from their troubles and anxieties into a world of whimsical nonsense.' That particular world could not survive without That Man's irrepressible spirit at the centre, and ITMA died with Tommy Handley.

This is their last tribute to a man who made them laugh

AGAIN it was Thursday—Tommy Handley's own day—ITMA day.

But it was a day of tears—not of laughter, for Radio, radio, as "Well, I don't wept.

For Tommy Handley, whose sudden death last Sunday shocked Britain, was dying on his last journey.

His cortege moved out miles of London's busy streets—grey streets, edged with the black mass of thousands of mourners—men, women and children.

With them, in feeling since millions of Tommy's closest friends, made in family years of broadcasts.

Their wreaths—a few dozen, a few handfuls, tied with ribbon (though there were many others with those great flowers which those three great ones in the cortege closed to Westminster—were Tommy Handley's.

JACK TRAIN ("Colonel Chinstrap") waiting for the funeral wreaths

From millions came flowers, saying "We shall miss you, Tommy." "Farewell From a Sorrow" ... To memory of many happy hours."

Crowds assembled in hundreds of silent offices, stood to form their tiny before the cortege of four hearses, three of them bearing flowers banked on their way to Golders Green Crematorium.

As it passed, bus drivers sat too in their hats ... the men of London sent aside, children waited in the silence closed ... and attended by many many and radio stars, the box whom John McDonnellI head of Variety Handley.

Diana Morrison ("Mrs. Mopp"), left, and Joan Harben ("Mona Lott")

"Bless his memory," he said the actor and the one who had given him his day. He has left behind him the radio House close to millions of listeners.

They gathered in their thousands—Tommy Handley's funeral procession starting from Westminster-green, London, yesterday.

But here the sightseers cheered, joked—and tore flowers from wreaths

By ROBERT GLENTON

Daily Mirror

ONE PENNY   No. 14,003

FRI. JAN. 14 1949

Registered at G.P.O. as a Newspaper

FORWARD WITH THE PEOPLE

ITMA fades out for the last time

THE NATION MOURNED ITS FIRESIDE FRIEND

TOMMY HANDLEY, jester to the people of Britain, was mourned yesterday by 12,000,000 people who knew him only as their fireside friend.

The last farewell to Tommy

They take along the line of thousands of people who yesterday came London streets to say farewell to "That Man."

6,000 people go to St. Paul's for the Tommy Handley service

The great congregation at more than 6,000 people crushing to honour St. Paul's Cathedral yesterday after the memorial service to former Handley service.

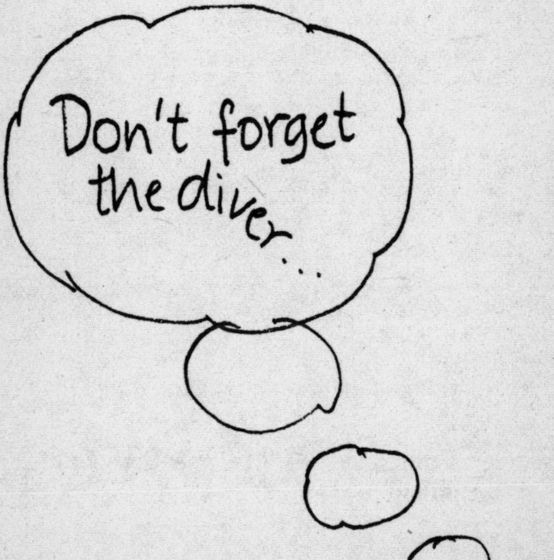
Don't forget the diver...

Printed by C. J. Mason & Sons Ltd.,
Bristol BS13 7TP.